Ex Libris

Florence G. Bailey

AMERICA'S RIDING HORSES

A GUIDE TO ALL BREEDS FOR THE AMATEUR

by

CAPTAIN HARRY P. ORCUTT, A.U.S. Ret.

AND

BEN AVIS ORCUTT

D. VAN NOSTRAND COMPANY, INC.

PRINCETON, NEW JERSEY

TORONTO   LONDON

NEW YORK

EDITED AND DESIGNED BY EUGENE V. CONNETT

PRINTED IN THE UNITED STATES OF AMERICA

D. VAN NOSTRAND COMPANY, INC.
120 Alexander St., Princeton, New Jersey (*Principal office*)
257 Fourth Avenue, New York 10, New York

D. VAN NOSTRAND COMPANY, LTD.
358, Kensington High Street, London, W.14, England

D. VAN NOSTRAND COMPANY (Canada), LTD.
25 Hollinger Road, Toronto 16, Canada

To My Wife

ACKNOWLEDGMENTS

My deepest appreciation to our horsemen and newspaper friends who helped me in completing my husband's book following his death. I am especially grateful to James D. Cary for help with writing, to Harry T. Montgomery for editorial advice, to Ivan Mashek for photography and to Janet Moone of Stephens College for reproductions of her art work.

MRS. BEN AVIS ORCUTT

Contents

List of Illustrations

CHAPTER I

Introduction

He stands stark and magnificent on the skyline. Mane whipped by the wind. Tail arched and flowing. Head high, eyes flashing and nostrils distended.

A picture of grace and poetry on a mountain top. A study of muscular harmony. A symphony of poised strength.

This is the horse at his best. A mental image of a lithe and beautiful animal that almost everyone has tucked away in some recess of his mind.

You admire him for his symmetry, for the ease with which he can break into sudden bursts of speed, make quick stops, abrupt turns, or go thundering up a rocky canyon, down a stream bed or race across a plain.

You love this companion and servant of man who has been present at some of the world's greatest moments, and you want to know more about him: how he can be made to perform for you; give you the smooth, rolling ride of the cavalier; perhaps take you sailing over a stone wall on a hunt, or maybe around a show ring before the admiring gaze of a crowded gallery.

But from whatever fount your interest springs, you have chosen well. There is probably no greater benefactor to man in his own way than the horse. He has carried our burdens and borne us across continents. He has fought in our wars and brought thrilling diversion to the thousands who have come to know him in his modern setting.

If you are a newcomer to the world of the horse, and perhaps even if you know something of his lore, there is much to learn about this great beast.

Where did he come from? What are the various breeds you hear mentioned so often? Why were they developed? How can you get a horse suitable for your purposes? And most of all how

1

should you take care of him and train him? What would you need to know to show him?

This book is written to answer those and many other related questions.

The earliest fossil remains of the horse are found in America, embedded in the great lacustrine formations of the Eocene geological period. They are spread over large areas of what is now New Mexico, Wyoming and Utah.

Yet, strangely enough, the modern horse had to be re-introduced in the Americas by the Spaniards. For the primitive equines, whose bones are embedded in many of our older rock formations, had been extinct for a long time when European civilization began to flow into the New World.

Fortunately for our story the horses that developed in Europe and Asia did not suffer a similar fate and Columbus, on his second voyage across the Atlantic, was able to bring 25 horses with him.

This was in 1493 and the location was the Island of Santo Domingo in the West Indies. The Spanish likewise brought horses into Mexico in 1519, and later into Florida in 1565.

The ancestry of these Spanish mounts is unknown, but they apparently had the blood of Arab horses and the Barb, the latter a horse of very mixed breeding, in their veins.

Streams of Spanish invasion and exploration moved both north and south from Mexico. Herds of wild horses developed and thrived in their new surroundings. Over the years, through selective breeding and the tapping of many bloodlines, great modifications took place and various types of horse, known as breeds, were developed, some in America and some in countries of the Old World, to be later transplanted to America.

Each breed has its own special attributes. For our purposes we will be largely concerned with the American Saddle Bred, Tennessee Walking Horse, the Arab, the Quarter Horse, the Morgan, Thoroughbred, Half-Bred and both Shetland and Welsh ponies.

The Arab, like so many early breeds, is of uncertain origin. Some claim he was developed thousands of years ago by the people of Arabia. Others say he was imported to Arabia from North Africa. And a third version is that he is related to the wild horses of Asia, a theory that many find hard to believe.

In any event, records of his breeding have been kept for nearly 5,000 years. He is considered the only *pure* breed of light horse in the world and is noted for his refined beauty, character, intelligence and kindly temperament.

The Thoroughbred was developed in England between 1616 and 1750 by breeding a number of now famous Arabs to English mares of mixed heritage. The breed was taken to what is now the United States in 1721.

The Half-Bred is a cross between the Thoroughbred and a so-called cold-blooded horse. Early crosses were such as the Cleveland Bay, Percheron, Clydesdale and Suffolk Punch.

The Quarter Horse is a unique American breed of running horse that is often used as a cowboy's mount. He was specifically bred for short distant races and derives his name from the quarter mile distance for which he is particularly suited.

The Quarter Horse stems from running horses developed in the southern states through a cross between the Florida-Spanish horse and early imported English racers. After the Civil War the Quarter Horse was introduced in Texas where he was crossed with the Spanish horse of the southwest.

The American Saddle Bred was developed in Kentucky late in the 18th century by mingling the blood of the Thoroughbred with work and general purpose or "stock-pot" horses.

The Morgan is of highly disputed ancestry, the controversy centering on Thoroughbred, Quarter Horse and Arab. But whatever his various blood-lines, he springs from a small bay colt acquired by Justin Morgan of Vermont in 1791. Deep of chest, sturdy, courageous and of great endurance, he was of a distinct type that was good for either harness or saddle. His blood runs in many types, including the Standardbred or American Trotting Horse.

The Tennessee Walking Horse has a history going back to the early settlement of Tennessee. Pioneers from Virginia and the Carolinas brought in what was considered an "all purpose horse" and crossed it with the Thoroughbred, Morgan, Standardbred and Saddle Bred to develop this very pleasant riding horse.

The Shetland and Welsh ponies both came from the British Isles.

With that very brief description of the various breeds and where they came from, we are ready to move on to the question of what horse is best suited for you. To aid in our explorations, the following list of terms may be of some help from time to time.

1. Amateur: One who rides or drives for pleasure rather than as a paid profession.
2. Common colors of Horses:
   BAY—Brown of varying shades with black mane and tail. He may have black lower extremities.
   BLACK
   CHESTNUT—Varying shades from gold to dark brown with mane and tail the color of body. A red chestnut is often called a sorrel.
   DUN—Varying from mouse color to silver with zebra-like stripes on body or legs.
   GRAY—A mixture of white hairs with the normal coat which occurs with advancing age.
   PALOMINO—Color of a newly minted gold coin with white mane and tail.
   ROAN—A mixture uniformly over the body of white and colored hairs.

PAINT—Irregular colored horse with white and any other color.

3. Markings:
   BLAZE—A broad white stripe from forehead to muzzle.
   RACE—A narrow white stripe from forehead to muzzle.
   SNIP—A small white mark between the nostrils.
   STAR—A small white spot on the forehead.
   STOCKINGS—White lower legs.
4. Breeds: Horses with peculiar characteristics of their own that reproduce their kind.
5. Gaits: Manner of moving. Different breeds have gaits peculiar to them. All horses naturally walk, trot and canter. Other gaits are pace, rack, slow-gait and running-walk.
6. Three-gaited: Refers to a Saddle Horse trained to perform with animation and action in the three gaits, walk, trot and canter.
7. Five-gaited: Refers to a Saddle Horse trained to perform in five gaits with animation and action, namely, the walk, trot, canter, slow gait and rack.
8. Action: This is lifting high and bending the knees and ankles as the horse makes a stride. The hind legs are also brought well up under the body.
9. Conformation: Body build or structure of a horse.
10. Foal: A new-born horse.
11. Dam: Mother of a foal.
12. Sire: Father of a foal.
13. Filly: A young female horse.
14. Colt: A young male horse.
15. Gelding: A castrated male horse unable to reproduce.
16. Unsoundness: A defect that renders the horse unable to function normally.
17. Blemish: A scar or other unsightly disfigurement that does not hinder the horse's usefulness.
18. Aids: Methods of signaling a horse, such as use of rider's legs, hands, voice or shift in body weight.
19. Equitation: The art of riding horseback.
20. To Show a Horse: This is the placing of a horse before an

audience to have him perform according to whatever training he has been given. A horse is shown in a show ring and judged on his qualities and performance as stipulated by the class in which he is competing. He may be judged on the way he executes his gaits, on his body structure, on how well he measures up to standards of his breed, the ease with which he is controlled and his ability to perform such feats as jumping, pivoting on his hind legs and many others.

21. Haute Ecole: Very advanced schooling of a horse in which the horse and rider appear to function as one. Intricate movements are requested of the horse wherein the rider's signals are imperceptible.

22. Lunge or Longe Line: This is a narrow web tape or line that is used in early schooling of a horse to teach obedience, or after he is trained, to exercise him. There is no rider. The line is fastened to the horse's halter and held by the trainer in such a manner as to cause him to move around the trainer in a circle.

23. English Saddle: A type of flat saddle used in park and show riding. The term is often used to distinguish this type of riding.

24. Western Horsemanship: The art of riding the Western type horse with a Western (that is one that has a horn) saddle.

25. Near Side: A horse's left side.

26. Off Side: A horse's right side.

27. Lameness: A condition of the legs or feet which causes a horse to limp or be completely crippled.

28. A Hand: Four inches. A horse's height is measured in hands.

CHAPTER II

The Horse Suitable for You

In selecting the horse suitable for you, it is necessary to decide whether you want him for pleasure, for showing or for hunting. All the different breeds of light horses may be shown or ridden for pleasure, but one will perform a particular job better than another, according to his breeding.

Therefore it is best to purchase a horse that is bred for the purpose for which you intend to use him. If you do this, you will find him a more pleasing mount and your job of training far easier.

The most ideal selection both for pleasure and show is the American Saddle Bred, or a horse with predominately Saddle Bred characteristics. The Saddle Bred is gentle, intelligent, superb in action and extremely pleasant to ride. His great beauty and performance have brought him the title of "the show horse."

Another top pleasure mount is the Tennessee Walker. He has become increasingly popular because of the great comfort he gives the rider with his gliding motion at the running walk.

The Arab and Quarter Horse are also fine horses for the person who rides just for the fun he gets out of it.

But when it comes to hunting or show jumping, most certainly the Thoroughbred and the Half-Bred are the best choices. Their structure or conformation endows them with tremendous strength for galloping and powerful muscular hindquarters that give the propulsion necessary to jump. Their leg structure enables them to endure the rough going on the hunt.

The Quarter Horse, Morgan, Percheron or Arab, bred to the Thoroughbred are also used as jumpers. The Saddle Bred, however, is not recommended for this purpose, although he can be taught to jump and makes a better hunter than some breeds.

The Arab, whose blood is in the foundation of all the breeds we have considered, is in a class by himself. He is by far the most versatile. He can be ridden with English or Western saddle, by adults or children, shown as a jumper or hunter and if desired can be made into a good cow pony. However, the Arab does not perform any of these tasks as well as the breeds which have been especially bred for their work. Hence, the Thoroughbred is a better hunter and jumper and a faster racer; the Saddle Bred is more desirable for the bridle path, and the Quarter Horse is better for herding stock.

Those riding Western saddle in the rocky Western States, like the Quarter Horse for his speed, docility, endurance and ability to perform as a stock horse. This does not mean that he necessarily works cattle. He may be trained as a stock horse performer and may never have seen a cow. The Thoroughbred is also being used increasingly in performing these arts. We will tell you more about this later.

A horse of riding type, but of no definite breed is called a "riding horse." He is generally of mixed breeding and his origin may be unknown. However, many authorities agree that a good "riding horse" ought to be as much as one-half Saddle Bred for a smooth, springy ride.

The Horse and Mule Association of America have estimated that the majority of riding horses in this country are not pure-bred animals of their breed, but grade horses produced by breeding mares of good riding horse type to pure-bred stallions and breeding their progeny again to pure-bred stallions. The resulting horses in characteristics are preponderantly Thoroughbred, Saddle Bred, Quarter Horse or whatever their sire. They are much less expensive than the pure-bred animal.

These various breeds which are commonly used for riding pleasure, for show or the hunt are explained more fully in Chapter III. Therefore, when we go on to suggest the horse most suitable for you, we are concerned with these breeds and with the "riding horse."

In selecting a horse, you should take time to look at the horses on hand in the stables or farms in your vicinity, for there are several things to be taken into consideration. First, as we have already indicated, you ought to have some idea of what you want him for.

Secondly, and doubtless the most important to many, is the price. Price will depend on how well trained or finished the horse

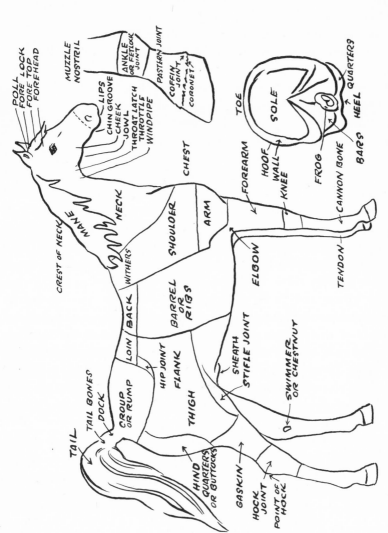

Fig. 1 Parts of a Horse.

is, his age, his bloodlines (heredity), the demand for his breed in your locality and his record of show winnings. To a certain extent, it must always be remembered that "you get what you pay for." Still, it is not exactly sensible for a novice to go out and buy an expensive show horse, or any other type that is near the finished product, unless he has a trainer or someone else more proficient than he to show the animal in the ring. Certainly, unless you are handicapped by some physical disability, you will want to ride your own horse.

This brings us to the third consideration, the degree of quality of your horsemanship. What are your capabilities as a rider? Will you be able to ride this horse? Is the horse more advanced or better trained than you are as a rider? Will he "go down" or will he improve under your tutelage?

A horse is schooled or taught as an individual. In his training process he learns that when his rider touches him on certain parts of his body, squeezes with his legs, shifts his weight in the saddle, or lets him feel light pressure of the bit, certain movements are expected of him. If you are only learning the fundamentals of riding, it is possible for you to ruin or harden the tender, responsive mouth of your finished or "educated" horse by handling the reins improperly. Thus these questions are important and should be definitely decided on before purchase.

The next thing to consider is the prospective purchaser's weight. Your weight and that of the horse should be in some relative proportion. A 200 pound man appears as awkward on a 14.3 hand horse as a child does on a 16.2 and makes the going even more difficult. A hand is four inches and the horse is measured from the point of the withers, which is just ahead of where the saddle rests, to the ground. (See Figure 1 for description of parts of the horse.)

A good suggestion in looking for a horse is to see the breeder before the trader if it is at all possible. The breeder usually has a larger selection and is apt to know his horse's manners and capabilities better than the trader, although some people complain that breeders and dealers ask higher prices at their stables than they will take later at a sale. You must be careful in any case to get value for your purchase. The trader often gets horses in trade that he is anxious to dispose of as soon as he can. This is not always the case but should be taken into consideration.

We know one large breeder who each year sells for $250.00, and less, the young horses that he does not believe to be top show winner prospects. Therefore, one may pick up a good pleasure horse, perhaps also suitable for show, at a reasonable figure.

Dealers and breeders advertise in the leading magazines that cater to the activities of their breeds, and you can easily locate breeders, sales and auctions in this way. A list of all horse magazines can be procured through the Magazine Mart, Plant City, Florida. The Tattersal Sales, Lexington, Kentucky, are among the country's largest for saddle horses.

Above all, go to a reputable dealer, breeder or trader—one whose guarantee will carry weight. Your horse must be guaranteed to be sound of eye, wind and limb, unless you are purchasing him with a known defect.

In buying, if you desire a good pleasure horse, one of six or seven years is a good age, but if at this age the cost is beyond your means, one a bit older will have to suffice. At seven, the horse has reached maturity and should be quiet and easily handled. However, if the horse is sound he may be good for pleasure or show far beyond this age. We know of a hunter twenty years old that is still winning hunter classes, and of others that have been broken down and are old at six years. Even with a show record, they sold cheap.

The novice cannot very well be expected to pick out the fine points of conformation or structure of a horse. So, for his ease of mind, we will state that the perfect horse has not yet been foaled. As far as conformation and soundness are concerned, if a defect is found after purchase, that is where your reputable dealer's guarantee will come in.

Of course different breeds of good horses to ride have different points of conformation. These differences in body-build enable them to do different tasks well. However, there are certain points to consider in picking any suitable horse.

From the head, which tells us most about the horse, we learn of his disposition and character. His head should be properly proportioned to his body. It should be lean, have a flat, wide forehead and eyes set far apart. The eyes should have a kind, friendly, intelligent expression. When they are set too close together, there is said to be less room for the brain and the horse is less intelligent. The ears should be small, not so far apart as to appear to come from the side of the horse's head. The head and neck are important to the animal's balance and if not well joined to the body, will hinder the horse in his gaits. The body should be compact, the ribs well-rounded and hindquarters broad and muscular. Notice whether there is sufficient slope from the withers and shoulders. This will help keep the saddle in place and he will also move easier in his gaits. The legs must be strong and sound, free of any disease or injury that may cause lameness or permanent loss of function.

There are many defects in horse's legs and feet, such as curb, thoroughpin, navicular disease and ringbone, that should not be overlooked and might not be detected by an amateur. Before buying, if possible, get the advice of a veterinarian or a competent horseman acquaintance, who is familiar with these bony enlargements, swellings and inflammations that may handicap or cripple a horse. Do not rely on your judgment alone.

These defects mentioned are only a few of the ailments that can beset a horse's legs and feet. Sir Frederick Hobday, in SADDLE UP, gives some very thorough explanations and illustrations on how to locate these defects. We are convinced that the best way to see and to know is to have a veterinarian or a good trainer go over a horse's legs with you, permitting you to see and feel the location of a splint by the heat and inflammation in the area, a wind-puff by the soft puffiness about the ankle or perhaps a bog-spavin by the enlargement of a hock ligament. These ailments often occur from working the horse too much when too young. Learning this way, you will remember these defects in the future.

Some defects can be corrected but others are either unsightly or permanently reduce the horse's usefulness. In Chapter IV, on Veterinary Remedies, there will be found more detail on these ailments.

A thorough examination of the tendons of the legs is necessary. Notice, too, while the horse is standing, if his legs are crooked or bowed at the knees as this may indicate whether he has been used too hard. Then have someone walk him away from you, turn him about and walk him back toward you. Now repeat at the trot. It is much easier in this way to notice lameness, a paddling way of movement, brushing of one foot against another, or whether the animal favors any one leg. Also notice any evidence of poor wind or impaired vision. Blindness can often be detected by moving your hand in front of the horse's eye.

If after inspection you find the horse is sound of leg, eye, wind, and is to your liking, and, if after ascertaining the price, you are still interested, ask to have him saddled and ridden for you. At this time you may note his obvious manners and vices if any. Notice if he stands quietly to be mounted, if he readily goes into his gaits and if he is easily handled and controlled by the rider. You will also want to know whether he is apt to nip at you, if he is a kicker in the stall, a cribber or a windsucker (horses that chew on the manger and swallow air). These vices are difficult to correct.

We suggest that you get from the seller, before purchasing, the horse's certificate of registration, if he is supposed to be registered. See that an unbroken chain of title is established to seller and that each ownership is attested to by the Secretary of the Breeders' Association and shows the breeding of the horse.

It is also wise to get a certificate from a veterinarian showing the horse's soundness of eye, wind and limb which can usually be had for the asking. If you wish these papers, be sure to get them before paying any money. After the sale has been made, they are very hard to obtain. These same arrangements can be made at an auction sale, as well as in a private transaction. At a sale, held by a reputable auction or sales company, the horses to be sold are always well described and a guarantee given by the consignor, backed by the sales company.

When buying a pony for a child, look for good conformation the same as if you were buying a horse for yourself. The pony must be absolutely trustworthy, sure-footed and have a "good mouth." The bars of the mouth on which the bit rests should be very tender, unless they have been hardened by rough pulling of the reins. The mouth has to be sensitive for the pony to respond to light pressure from the bit. A good mouth is not only desirable for equitation but for safety.

FIG. 2   This five-year-old western rider is quite at home on his pony and shows that he has worked hard for his first ribbon.

Five years is a good age at which to start the child to ride. In selecting his pony, try to get one as narrow as possible in order that the child's legs may not be strained too much and he will have a better chance to grip with his knees. It is better to let a child select the size of his pony. Chances are that he will select one under-size rather than over-size. That is all right, for he will have far more confidence in beginning to ride if he feels that the pony is not too large. An older pony is also preferable to a younger one if he has a "good mouth."

The Shetland pony is most frequently used in this country both for riding and driving. However, some Welsh ponies are used, as well as the Chincoteague, found along the Virginia coast. Any of the breeds of riding horses we have mentioned that do not develop beyond 14.2 hands in height are considered as ponies. Small pony Thoroughbreds, Arabs, and Welsh, as well as crosses of these breeds make good hunters and jumpers for children.

If your child is given a pony, it is well at the beginning that he take care of the pony himself. Habits of this nature formed early in life will stay with the child and bring about a closer bond between pony and rider.

Instruction should proceed slowly so that the child will gain confidence. Take no chance of a spill that might later make the child afraid. A competent teacher of horsemanship is absolutely necessary; but if no teacher is available, a book by Mrs. Jane M. Dillon, SCHOOL FOR YOUNG RIDERS, is a very helpful substitute.

CHAPTER III

Breeds to Ride, Show or Hunt

To help you select the breed or the horse most suitable to your tastes and needs, we will discuss each of the breeds generally used for riding pleasure, for show and for hunters. We will also review horses known for their color.

For Pleasure on the Bridle Path and Show

The AMERICAN SADDLE BRED is the most beautiful of all horses. He is not only THE SHOW horse, but also the finest pleasure mount. This animal, a descendant of the Thoroughbred *Denmark,* can be gaited, mounted or driven for pleasure or show. He can also be used as a road hack, trail horse, low hurdle jumper and in some cases ridden to hounds.

Sometimes a Saddle Bred horse is confused with a "riding horse." The Saddle Bred is a distinct breed, as are the Thoroughbred and Percheron. A horse used for saddle purposes, but not of any specific breed, is a "riding horse." The Saddle Bred originated in Kentucky and was once known, and even now is sometimes referred to, as the Kentucky Saddle Bred.

The Saddle Bred horse is gentle, willing and alert, has animation and brilliance, and speed and action in performance. His many attributes have been bred in him for generations, not only for speed and action but for conformation. By action we mean the characteristic stride in which he lifts his front and hind feet very high, flexing or bending his knees and ankles. This gives him a striking, showy appearance and you a better ride. Notice his action in the pictures of the American Saddle Bred, Figures 3 and 4.

In Thoroughbreds, Morgans, Arabs and other breeds, the points of quality vary with the breed. We believe one must have more to reach the "top horse" class in the Saddle Bred than in any of the others. Conformation and animation are secondary qualities in

Fig. 3   Three-gaited American Saddle Bred—mane and tail are cut.

FIG. 4 Five-gaited American Saddle Bred—flowing mane and tail.

the Thoroughbred. If the Thoroughbred or Standardbred (trotter or pacer) can cross the finish line first, they win. That is not true with the Saddle Bred.

If you want to use him as a "show horse," here are some of the things you should look for. Beginning at the top:

He must have well set ears, a small lean head, should be wide and flat between the eyes and the eyes should be large, bold and well placed. These are signs of his good disposition and intelligence.

He must have large nostrils and thin lips and muzzle. His entire head and neck carried high, should have a look of fineness and elegance. He must also have a wide chest, short body from elbow to stifle, lean tapering neck, well-rounded ribs, slanting shoulders and rounded croup. His legs and feet must be sound, the hocks and knees without fat or blemishes. He must have long pasterns set at the proper angle with the hoof. The hindquarters of a good Saddle Bred show horse are broad and muscular and he does not droop to the tail. The tail, mane and forelock, unless clipped for the three gaits, must be long and flowing.

Show horses, whose tails are not naturally set high on the body, are made to stand straight and high by "tail-setting." The small tendons under the tail are clipped in such a way that when they heal, they are slightly longer than before they were severed. The tail is then set in a device called a crupper, fastened to a light body harness to hold it in place. After the tail has healed, the crupper is removed and worn only a few days before shows. Horses being shown regularly usually wear it through the show season. It may, however, be worn night and day and the horse may even lie down and roll with it.

There has been much controversy regarding the practice of tail-setting, but it is commonly used on horses for show in this breed and others. We quote from a letter written by Col. C. J. Cronan, Jr., Secretary of the American Saddle Horse Breeders' Association, published a few years ago: "One of the main desires of horsemen in setting tails is to get them straight. A crooked tail not very noticeable in a riding horse, would be objectionable in the show ring. After tails are straightened and raised . . . we get the desired effect of a handsomely carried tail, only artificial in that it

gives the chance to look as handsome as the chosen few whom
nature has blessed. Please be informed that in setting horse's tails,
the tail is not broken at any point. After the operation, the horse
has just as complete and powerful use of his tail as he had before
the operation."

To complete the picture, the Saddle Bred must be intelligent
and have a fine way of going. By way of going—we mean the way
he travels in performing his various gaits.

The Saddle Bred is catalogued into different classifications according to his use and the way he travels. He is classified as a gaited
horse, fine harness or pleasure horse.

To be gaited, he must be able to go with form and action in
either three or five different gaits. The gaits natural to him are the
walk, trot and canter. The three-gaited horse is trained in only
these gaits. The two additional, unnatural gaits of the five-gaited
horse are slow gait and rack. They must be developed. Three and
five-gaited horses may not compete against each other at shows.
The custom of roached (trimmed) mane for the three-gaited is to
prevent them being shown out of class.

At the walk the Saddle Bred must pick up his feet with energy,
carry them over in a straight line from one point of contact to the
next. The joints, knees and ankles must bend, while the hocks
should be carried well under his body. His walk must express
vigor and be lively, with a stride of reasonable length, in keeping
with the size of the horse. Each foot makes a distinct sound as it
hits the ground in a one, two, three, four beat.

At the trot, called a diagonal two beat gait, the foreleg and diagonal hind leg advance simultaneously in making the stride. There
should be balance of the body, elasticity and straightness of motion. The flexing of the joints should be more noticeable than in
the walk.

The five-gaited Saddle Bred, especially the show type, must
have speed as well as form. Lack of hock action is objectionable.
Notice the form and action at the trot in Figures 3, 4 and 6.

The canter, a three beat gait, is executed either with a left lead
or a right lead. That is, the horse advances either with the left or
right foreleg slightly higher and ahead of the other leg. This happens because the motion at the gait begins from his diagonal hind

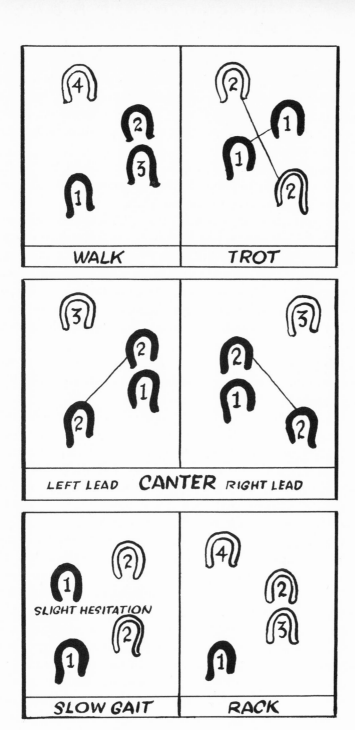

Fig. 5 Illustration of gaits.

leg, followed by the other pair of diagonally opposed legs striking the ground together. Thus the final beat occurs with the foreleg reaching out ahead. Since the first and third beats are each made with a single leg, the gait has a rocking motion.

Do not confuse this gait with the gallop for it is much slower, though the foot movements are similar. The stride of the Saddle Bred at the canter should be of reasonable length and not too high. Also, a reasonable amount of speed is necessary with agility, yet the feet should not hit the ground too hard.

The gaited horse is not allowed to gallop or push on from the canter. If the Saddle Bred is used as a road hack in cross country riding, he may go at this faster gait.

The slow gait being unnatural, is developed by training and practice. It must be done gracefully and with rhythm and precision. The right hind foot, right forefoot and the left hind foot and left forefoot strike the ground as distinct beats, in that order. The horse is gathered (at attention), holding his head high and well flexed, with the rider exerting enough pressure on the reins to keep him slow with a maximum of action. His speed will be about equal to a slow trot at this gait.

The rack involves still a different movement. It is also a four beat gait with each foot striking the ground at a separate time. Beginning with the first beat of the left hind foot, the right forefoot makes the second beat, the right hind foot the third beat, and the left front foot the fourth beat. It is a broken pace. This gait must be performed with ease and grace and ample height to the stride but with form and action still maintained. There must also be as much speed as possible. This is one of the finest gaits, but is tiring and should not be maintained over long distances.

Followers of other breeds maintain that the Saddle Bred wastes too much energy through excessive action, but it is this very thing that makes his way of going beautiful and his ride more pleasant.

Speed is not as necessary for the three-gaited horse as it is for the five-gaited animal when moving at the rack or trot. The three-gaited trot should not exceed 12 miles per hour. However, both horses must show much animation and brilliance which contributes to their elegance in the show ring.

The Saddle Bred classed as a fine harness horse must be five-

gaited in type, with long mane and tail. However, he is not required to be able to go in five gaits, though he may be. He is
shown driven to a light four-wheeled fine harness buggy. In the
ring he does a brilliant animated walk and park trot (slow trot
with much form and action) . See Figure 6.

Both three-gaited and five-gaited Saddle Breds may be shown
in combination classes at the walk and trot, then unhitched and
saddled while still in the ring and shown in the three or five gaits.

The Saddle Bred classed as a pleasure horse goes at his natural
stride in the three basic gaits, walk, trot and canter. The form and
action we see in the gaited horse are absent.

You will say "no horse has all these qualities." Perhaps not, but
that is the goal which breeders of the Saddle Bred are seeking and
they are getting closer to it each year.

You do not necessarily have to be wealthy to own a Saddle Bred.
Top registered show horses with the points of conformation we
have described and winning records are naturally expensive.
However, a grade Saddle Bred without a finished education may
be better for you to start with as a novice, or to train yourself, if
you are a proficient rider. You can buy them for prices ranging
down to less than $500.00, depending on the horse and locality.
Even a finished horse of good pedigree may sell cheaper if he is
older or blemished. If you plan to show your horse, blemishes
will count against you in the ring; however, they will not affect
your pleasure on the bridle path.

The TENNESSEE WALKING HORSE, also a fine breed for
pleasure and show, is becoming increasingly popular throughout
the United States. The "Walker's" greatest popularity, however,
is in the Southeast where he originated.

This breed was developed about 100 years ago, and in 1935 the
Tennessee Walking Horse Breeders' Association of America was
formed in Lewisburg, Tennessee, to preserve and record the
breed. He is often referred to as the Plantation Horse as presum-
ably his forebears developed the running walk from being ridden
over plowed fields by overseers in the Old South. Even today, being bred primarily for pleasure and show, trainers school him
over plowed furrows to aid in developing the over-reach in stride
for which he is famous.

Fɪɢ. 6   American Saddle Bred in Fine Harness.

Foundation stock producing this breed include the Thoroughbred, Saddle Bred, Standardbred and Morgan crossed with native Tennessee mares.

In conformation the Tennessee Walking Horse differs from the Saddle Bred in that he is plainer in appearance, with a somewhat thicker head and neck and a more weighty, powerful body. He ordinarily stands 15 to 16 hands, has large muscular hindquarters, strong legs, with a deep, well-developed chest. His shoulders are well-muscled and sloping which aids him in his gaits. Like the Saddle Bred, his tail is also set if he is to be shown, to give him a more handsome appearance.

His distinguishing feature, and cause of his great popularity, is his running walk. He is bred for this gait and it is exceedingly comfortable to ride. People past middle-age often prefer the breed for this reason.

When in shape he does three gaits, a flat-foot walk, running walk and canter on both leads. His walk is diagonal and "square" with a bold, hard-hitting definite four beat sound. The running walk is the same diagonal motion of the fore and hind feet but a faster, extended gait in which the hind foot overlaps the print of the forefoot on the same side. Slow motion pictures show the front foot striking the ground an instant before the diagonal hind foot. Therefore three feet are on the ground at any one time. Thus the horse has a gliding motion and the rider barely feels any movement in the saddle. This contrasts to the up and down motion of the trot which calls for posting by the rider.

In order to get the horse into a good extended running walk, he has to be warmed up for several minutes from the walk. The Association rules state that when he goes into the show ring that he must go at a running walk and the way he performs this gait is more to his credit than his conformation or other two gaits.

The overreach of his hind feet was formerly about 12 inches, but trainers in the Southeast have been working on this, and according to the Breeders' Association, the average has now increased to 36 inches. Some boast of overreach up to 100 inches with speed of 16 miles an hour. At this speed the horse is probably not walking but tending to paddle, trot, pace or even rack. The ultimate goal is to get speed comparable to the Saddle Bred. *Talk*

Of The Town, world champion Tennessee Walker, is said to have an overstride of five feet.

Front action is desired in the Walking Horse but no hock action, as this would prevent his long overstride and walk. (Notice the difference in use of the hind legs in pictures of the Saddle Bred and Walking Horse in Figure 7.) In appearance the Walking Horse must flick his ears, chomp on his bit, nod his head and really walk to be genuine.

The canter is sometimes called his "rocking chair" gait. It is executed on both leads similar to the canter in other breeds, but there is a slight rolling motion which makes the rider feel as though he were in a rocking chair.

As an amateur you could not choose a horse with better disposition or that will give you more pleasure. However, you should be careful in the selection of this breed, being sure to get a Walker that performs his gaits naturally. Those which have had so much development and training for overreach and speed, generally have to be ridden by a trainer who is skilled in making them function at their best. Otherwise, the amateur will find he has too much horse and cannot get him to move easily in his gaits. A true Walker will do his running walk as a young foal and this gait need only be perfected.

The breed is in much demand and, as in the case of the Saddle Bred, those with show records and prospective winners are expensive. Yet we have seen an older, registered, pleasure horse sell for less than $100.00. Your price will depend on the horse and some of the high priced horses are not winners.

The ARAB is a more versatile breed than the others. It may well be your choice for the bridle path, the trail or for use as a hunter or jumper. (More will be said of this latter use later.) They are easy keepers, which means they will maintain their weight and strength on comparatively small amounts of grain and hay. This makes them particularly useful in range country.

The Arab runs smaller than other breeds and because of his good disposition and tractibility is often used as a children's mount. He has one less vertebra in his back than other horses and even though most Arabs do not top 15 hands, their stride is proportionately greater than that of any other breed. The Arab is not a

Courtesy Mrs. Harold P. Moore and Mrs. Gene Eaton Schuff

Fɪɢ. 7 Tennessee Walking Horse.

Fig. 8   The Arab Horse, *Indraff*.

natural trotter, but gallops at a more extended gait. His gallop involves the same foot movement we described in the canter but it is much faster, with an extension of the legs in making the stride. He can also execute a fast walk, overreaching with the hind foot, and can be taught the five gaits of the American Saddle Bred. Though his action is inferior, he performs admirably when shown.

His endurance and stamina are remarkable; he may be found working cattle at 10,000 feet altitude. His depth of chest, wide girth and large windpipe enable him to function at altitudes even up to 13,000 feet.

The Arab, like the Saddle Bred, has a certain elegance and fineness of the head, though his conformation is very different. His lips and muzzle are thin, his head short with eyes wide apart, and set about half-way from his muzzle to the top of his head. He has a dished face and often a broad stripe from the forehead to the muzzle called a blaze. He is as high at the croup as at the withers and looks nearly even across the top. His legs are short and his pasterns slope well to the hoof. He has a lot of fire and courage and is known as a hot-blooded horse, though he is gentle and affectionate. He makes a flashy saddle mount and carries his tail naturally high.

If crossed with the Saddle Bred mare, the probable "get" would be reduced size and bad type, although it might produce an excellent horsemanship mount for young riders, a bridle path hack or a fair jumper.

The Arab is actually not a specialist for any of the pleasure uses we have talked about, yet he will afford you much pleasure in whatever capacity you use him. There are many all-Arab shows over the country, as well as Arab classes where he may compete with his own breed as a park horse or as a pleasure horse under Western saddle or English flat saddle. As a park horse he does a walk, trot and canter with animation and brilliance resembling the Saddle Bred. As a pleasure horse he is ridden with reasonably loose rein, and pushes on into the gallop if required in his classes.

Because of the Arab's stamina he is a pleasure on the trails. He can endure the rough going up and down ditches, embankments or through muddy bogs. The Arab may also be hitched and driven.

There has been great interest throughout the country in recent years to preserve this foundation breed and purebred Arabs are expensive. However, if you are attracted to the breed, you may do as some others, use him as your pleasure horse in any capacity you like and, if a mare, breed her occasionally. Her foals will ordinarily bring you a good price as Arab blood is used to improve quality in other horses.

The QUARTER HORSE, though essentially a 400 yard racer, makes a good all-around pleasure mount, particularly if you ride Western saddle. He is most often trained as a stock horse; however, he is becoming increasingly popular all over the United States as a pleasure horse. His general upkeep runs less than some other breeds and he is quiet and easily handled. He may be used as a racer, a working cow horse or strictly for pleasure or show.

We have heard numerous anecdotes as to how and where the Quarter Horse originated, how he derived his name, that he can out-run the Thoroughbred and he is the best cow horse in the world. There is doubtless more lore connected with the Quarter Horse than any other today. We can say he is a descendant of colonial days, when English Thoroughbreds were crossed with native Spanish ponies and raced over a quarter mile.

In every corner of the country natives have chosen one breed of horse as having ideal qualities for work, competitive contests and personal riding pleasure. Throughout the Southwest few persons would question the popularity of the Quarter Horse. The animal can be used for ranchwork during the week, raced on Sunday or ridden over the desert in the evening.

The Quarter Horse is a much plainer looking horse than the other breeds we have described. He is smaller, usually 14 to 15 hands, has a short heavily muscled body with a sloping rump. He is low to the ground with short legs, short pasterns and small feet. Large joints in his legs are not objectionable. He has plenty of width through the chest for lung capacity and very pronounced sloping shoulders. His head is short with a thicker muzzle, heavy rounded jowls and short ears.

He moves out at a gallop while other horses are only getting in stride and turns on his hind feet at a gallop with equal ease. He is tough and able to go at excessive speed over short distances. His quiet, docile disposition, his intelligence and hardiness, make him

Fɪɢ. 9   The Quarter Horse.

Courtesy The Morgan Horse Club, Inc.

FIG. 10   The Morgan Horse.

an ideal pleasure or trail horse, especially over rocky terrain. For show he is also trained as a performer of stock horse arts, turning and spinning on his hind feet, backing and coming to a sliding stop.

The Quarter Horse is commonly ridden for show or pleasure under Western saddle. This sport is not limited to the West, as there are numerous opportunities for riding Western style in the Eastern part of the United States. In 1953 the American Horse Shows Association had listed 36 shows by mid-summer with 130 Western classes at points east of the Mississippi River. They reported many of them in Northern New York State. They were also very popular in New England and New Jersey. This does not include the many shows put on by non-members of the Association.

As a pleasure mount the Quarter Horse is shown in three gaits—walk, trot and lope on the correct lead. The lope is a medium fast canter. He is ridden with a loose rein.

The MORGAN is another excellent long distance trail horse and a fine pleasure mount. Many Morgans are today competing in American Saddle Bred shows and giving a good account of themselves. The modern Morgan is bred mostly for saddle purposes and breeders have infused some Saddle Bred blood. Years ago he was used as a utility horse for transporation via saddle or buggy.

The size of the Morgan varies. The animal is stocky, usually runs 15 hands and weighs one-half ton. He is a much plainer horse than the American Saddle Bred but similarly carries his head high and has a good disposition. His muscular body portrays his strength and stamina, and his legs are strong with short cannons and sloping pasterns. Old *Justin Morgan,* his progenitor, stood 14.2 and weighed 1,100 pounds. He was foaled the latter part of the 18th century in Vermont and was of Arab-Barb descent. He passed on his fine qualities regardless of the attributes of the mares.

Unlike the Tennessee Walker and American Saddle Bred, the Morgan is shown with his natural tail carriage in classes devoted to his breed. He may be shown either under saddle or in harness. His gaits are walk, trot and canter when ridden. In fine harness he goes at an animated walk and park trot. When shown in three-gaited and harness classes his high natural action is exhibited, but as a pleasure horse and hack, he goes with a more extended and natural stride. His strength and ability to cover ground make him a superior trail horse.

Mustangs and Colored Horses

Range horses of the West are descendants of the Mustangs and other Spanish horses brought to the Southwest by the early Spanish settlers. They lived in a wild state on the range and authorities say their blood was blended with the Arab from California as well as the Thoroughbred, Quarter Horse, Morgan and other breeds the pioneers brought West. The descendants of these range horses, gentled and trained, make good pleasure horses of Western type that do not require expensive upkeep. The Army Remount Service has sought to improve them in recent years with Thoroughbred blood. They do not have the uniform points of conformation nor the fineness and physical style of the more specialized breeds, but provide you with a good pleasure mount at little expense.

You can show them in Western pleasure events with full knowledge that their style will have little to do with whether they win. Their manners and performance will count the most. Their quality and strength next. However, if you show them as trail horses, conformation will count 20 percent in most shows. Range horses gaits are walk, trot and lope with a natural extended stride. The beginning horseman should be warned that if the horse's pasterns are straight and short, his gaits will be choppy and rough to ride.

Indians used slective breeding of Mustangs and their descendants to produce horses of varied colors. Most popular among them are the PINTOS or PAINTS. They are irregular colored horses of white and black (Piebalds) and white and brown or any other color (Skewbalds). They are generally 14 to 15 hands and children as well as adults are attracted to them because of their appearance.

Paints are often found among Shetland ponies and may show up in Thoroughbreds, Quarter Horses or other breeds, when colored horses are in their heritage.

FIG. 11 The Pinto or Paint—an irregular colored horse.

The APPALOOSA is also a colored horse that is considered a breed of his own. He is not widely known and is found mostly in the West. He is generally used as a working cow horse but may be ridden for pleasure or shown in cow horse events.

He may have found his way to this country through Mexico. Some believe traders in the Mediterranean sold spotted horses that were cargoed both to England and to Mexico. The Appaloosa is characterized by spots on his rump. In ancient times he was known as the "blood sweating" horse. He has a spotting of pink and black skin in small irregular proportions and a thin mane and tail.

The most popular of all the colored horses and favorite with many on the trails, as well as for shows and parade, is the PALOMINO. He is not generally considered a breed of his own but a color. However, the Palomino Breeders of America, Inc., have been working toward establishing the Palomino as a breed. They have now set up a separate registration to qualify for the breed. The separate registration is called Palomino Breed Registry.

To qualify for the Breed Registry by pedigree, the sire or dam, or both, must be registered Palomino. If either is not registered, it must qualify on bloodline, such as Quarter Horse, Arab or Thoroughbred. To qualify by progeny, a stallion must have five of his get registered in Palomino Regular Registry, or a mare must be Palomino herself and have three of her produce registered. The color must be that of a newly minted gold coin, varying only three shades to light, medium or dark, with pure white mane and tail, varying to silver and flaxen. He must have dark eyes and have no Shetland or draft blood, nor piebald or albino parents.

Some proponents of the Palomino as a breed claim he descended from animals brought to this country by Cortez. However, most authorities hold the opinion that the Palomino is not a definite breed of his own but a color. He is a Saddle Bred, Tennessee Walker, Quarter Horse, Morgan, Thoroughbred or whatever blood he may carry. The Palomino has been produced in almost every known breed. Thus, there continues to exist the Regular Registry or double registration for the Palomino. One registration is with the Palomino Horse Breeders of America as to color, and the other with the Association of the breed to which he belongs. Indicative of his growing popularity is his show adoption by the

American Horse Shows Association and the setting up of a separate classification for Palominos with specific qualifications for judges.

Palominos are judged on color and conformation, that is, as to trueness of the type being shown and conformation resembling to a marked degree that of animals listed in a given registry. Thus, if he is a Quarter Horse in conformation and registry, he is judged for Quarter Horse conformation and Palomino color.

Breeds Commonly Used as Hunters, Jumpers and Hacks

We come now to the Blue Blood of the horse world—the THOROUGHBRED. Either he or the Half-Bred is the best mount for show jumping. The Arab on occasions has distinguished himself as a jumper but he does not have the conformation or the power to outdo the Thoroughbred. Most authorities agree that to show your hunter in conformation hunter classes, you almost have to have a Thoroughbred to win. Hunting and jumping enthusiasts often use a three-fourths or seven-eighths thoroughbred or a Half-Bred to combine the conformation and strength of the Thoroughbred with a less temperamental, more docile breed.

The Thoroughbred is primarily known as a race horse. He is the swiftest of any breed. First and last he is bred for speed and when not used in racing is trained for hunting, jumping and polo. In addition to these uses, Thoroughbreds make excellent bridle path hacks and High School horses. They are strong and tractable and will gallop intermittently from 10 to 30 miles over rough country on a foxhunt and have as much fun as you.

Historians who trace the Thoroughbred's origin, note that Queen Elizabeth I and Charles II of England imported Arabs and Barbs for their royal races. Between 1690 and 1750 three famous Arabs, *Godolphin Arabian, Darley Arabian* and *Byerley Turk* were among the imports. They were crossed with cold-blooded native English mares, producing the Thoroughbred. All Thoroughbreds must descend from these three stallions. In turn the Thoroughbred founded other breeds among which are the Saddle Bred and Quarter Horse.

The Thoroughbred is tall and usually stands 15 to 17 hands in height. He is wide and deep in the chest. His hindquarters are powerful and muscular, providing the propulsion he needs in

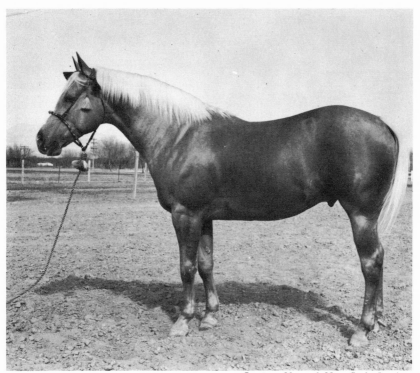

Courtesy Mr. and Mrs. Gayle Jennings

FIG. 12 The Palomino—Color of a newly minted gold coin with white mane and tail. The above horse has double registration, one with the Palomino Breeders of America, Inc., and one with the Quarter Horse Breeders' Association. Notice his Quarter Horse conformation.

FIG. 13   The Thoroughbred. *Tom Fool.*

jumping. His well sloped shoulders aid in getting his forelegs off the ground and in absorbing the shock when he lands. They also make him an easy galloper and he goes with an extended low stride. The high action we saw in the Saddle Bred is absent. His legs are long with flat appearing joints.

The tail comes out high on his body and is carried naturally. The Thoroughbred's head is not so tapered or small as the Saddle Bred nor does he have the stylish animation. But he is not bred for these qualities; his fame is in his speed on the flat, his courage, and heart in taking jumps and moving across country.

In character, the Thoroughbred is temperamental with a restless energy. His body is very sensitive to touch and consequently he is easily trained to jump and to execute intricate body movements as in Haute Ecole.

His gaits are walk, trot and canter with a natural ability to move on at a gallop. His head is generally carried low and his way of going is extended and natural.

Hunters are divided into four classes: (1) Small—not exceeding 15.2½ hands; (2) Lightweight—able to carry up to 165 pounds; (3) Middleweight—able to carry up to 185 pounds; (4) Heavyweight—able to carry up to 205 pounds. Speed is not needed so much as endurance, strength and power. The weight your animal can carry is determined by the measurement of his leg bone just below the knee. The larger the circumference, the more weight he can carry. A lightweight hunter usually measures about eight inches, a middleweight eight to eight and one-half and heavyweight eight and one-half to nine and over. The heavyweight Thoroughbred is not prevalent and sportsmen often try various crosses to get the right weight carrier. Heavyweights often have draft blood. Some persons also prefer Half-Breds. Therefore, to get the right weight carriers and temperament, crosses are often made with the Cleveland Bay, Quarter Horse, Range Horses, Morgan, Hackney, Percheron and other breeds. They may make useful, less sensitive, slower hunters, while crosses with the Arab may give more speed to the progeny of an animal of fine appearance and stamina. Pure Arab hunters and jumpers are often used by children.

The hunter, whose primary purpose is to take you safely across country when hunting, must not only be suitable to your weight but amenable to your will. He must be so trained that he can be stopped at will when sudden danger confronts you, either over fences or in the field.

Foxhunting has long been a popular sport in England and naturally was followed in this country as it was settled. Today foxhunting is still most popular along the Eastern Seaboard and inland, although the Far West has nine and the Mid-West seventeen established Hunts. Hunts are established and recognized by the Masters of Foxhounds Association of America, located in Boston. Each Hunt must be chartered and abide by certain standards. This organization is to hunting what the American Horse Shows Association is to showing.

Not all hunts are recognized and established by this organization. Many foxhunts are staged by a group of townsmen who want a chance to gallop with hounds, more or less informally.

The average show ring hunter has probably never seen a hound. He is trained to jump obstacles of the same type he would meet in the hunting field, such as post and rail fence, rockwall, and brush. He must show ability to go at a hunting pace, taking obstacles in stride and galloping on. His style and form as well as his conformation are important if he is being shown as a conformation hunter. However, if you are showing him as a working hunter, his conformation is not considered. Then he is judged on whether he is agreeable to hounds, his way of going, performance and hunting soundness.

Riding your hunter in his gaits is called hacking. Horse shows generally offer classes to show him under saddle at his gaits and may require him to take two jumps in addition.

The Thoroughbred and Half-Bred are also commonly used as show jumpers. A jumper should be physically agile. He jumps higher and wider obstacles than the hunter. It doesn't matter about his jumping form as long as he scales the jump without touching. He must have plenty of strength and power for such gymnastics.

Freudy Photo

Fig. 14   A Thoroughbred Jumper, *Riviera Wonder,* winning the Waldorf-Astoria Challenge Trophy for the second year at Madison Square Garden.

Ponies for Children

You do not have to be grown-up to enjoy riding, hunting or show jumping. A child can ride a pony suitable to the task and perform as well as his elders do.

For classification, a pony is any member of the horse family under 14 hands. For show purposes and polo players, it has been stretched to 14.2.

Probably the best known and most widely used pony is the SHETLAND. He is generally a child's pet, is docile, gentle and affectionate. He usually ranges from 40 to 46 inches in height. One of the smallest on record was 26 inches. The Shetland is a hardy, stocky animal with strong heart and somewhat draft-like appearance. His miniature size is believed to have resulted from generations of bare existence on the Shetland Isles, off the coast of Scotland. In America, the Shetland has been improved so much by selective breeding that he is a much more beautiful animal than his cousin in his native land.

Shetlands that are not so well bred are shaggy and knotty in appearance. Those that are better bred are sleek, have short heads and bodies, well-shaped flat legs, thin muzzle, short ears and are even across the back.

The Shetland is schooled in the walk, trot and canter, but his training is often not as finished as that of the horse. He may be ridden for pleasure or driven, hitched to a light cart. When driven, his way of going is similar to the American Saddle Bred in fine harness. Shetlands are crossed with Hackneys to get larger ponies and fine driving style. For show, these crosses should not exceed 48 inches.

The WELSH pony runs larger than the Shetland but is not as prevalent in this country. He is a native of Wales as his name suggests. He is trained successfully as a hunter, jumper and hack. He is intelligent and his way of going is more like that of a horse. A cross with the Arab also makes a fine jumper.

For show purposes, hunter ponies are classed as small ponies, 11.2 hands and under; medium ponies over 11.2 and not over 13 hands; and large ponies, over 13 hands and not exceeding 14.2. Small ponies 11.2 and under do not jump over two feet.

Children make quite a spectacle driving their miniature Shetlands with miniature carts, as well as jumping their hunters in hunt attire. They too, along the Eastern Seaboard, have organized Hunts under the direction of the Senior Hunts. They use the Senior Hunt's country and hounds.

All breeds of horses we have described that are suitable to ride, show or hunt, occasionally produce foals that do not develop beyond 14.2 hands and are therefore ponies. A Thoroughbred or Arab pony will make an ideal hunter or jumper. Youngsters can also have the same fun as their elders with a Saddle Bred, Tennessee Walker or Hackney pony to ride or drive for show or pleasure.

The CHINCOTEAGUE pony that runs wild along the Virginia coast also makes a good riding pony when he is broken and gentled. A few CONNEMARAS have been imported to Virginia but they are draft-like and not in wide enough use to merit discussion.

Courtesy Emily Albritton and A. M. Bullard Farms

FIG. 15   The Shetland Pony has long been a favorite with children.

CHAPTER IV

Stable Management

In stable management, the first consideration is the stable itself. If you are planning to build a barn or stable, the suggestions contained herein will be helpful. If you are looking for a barn to purchase or rent, or one in which to board your horse, these pointers will make your decision easier.

The size stable you need will, of course, depends on whether you have one or several horses. They are generally built on two plans. One has a center passageway with stalls on either side. The other has a single line of adjacent stalls with an overhanging, porch-like, roof, covering the outside passageway. This latter type is more economical and advisable if you have only one or two horses. See Figures 16 and 17.

A stable is a useful but not indispensable means of protection. The animal in his natural state is able to withstand low temperatures. This has been proved in Russia during their very cold, below zero, winters. It is well known that if horses are protected from drafts and dampness, well fed, given a good clean bed and blanketed according to the season, they will thrive, even if the temperature of the barn is as cold as a Northern Michigan winter. Heated stables are not practical. Where examinations of horses in heated stables have been made, invariably most of the animals were suffering from colds.

It is important that the barn be light, airy, dry and clean. All windows should be open except those that might cause drafts. In cold weather, the windows can be opened on the sheltered side of the barn.

All in all, a stable should interfere as little as possible with those natural conditions that are conducive to the health and comfort of a horse. Heat promotes contamination of the air. Moisture and heat together encourage vermin and disease. Purity of air in stables is probably the most important factor in the health of the horse.

When building a barn or stable, we suggest a location where the soil is dry and well drained. If possible, build by the side of a hill, for that will serve as a wind breaker. A southerly or southwest exposure is most desirable in order to get sunshine in the barn. The sun is very beneficial to the health of any horse.

Also select a place where there is some land that can be converted into a pasture and a place where you can either build a ring or have a good dirt road on which to school your horses. Be sure that you have access to fresh water, and if you are a trail rider be careful that you do not have to ride through a town to get to the woods. Perhaps the most important admonition of all, especially in foxhunting country—be absolutely sure that you will like your neighbors and they will like you. Nothing can harass you more than unsympathetic neighbors who will not tolerate your crossing their property.

Special attention must be given to drainage, inside the barn as well as outside. If moisture is not efficiently carried away, it will create unhealthy stenches. Many satisfactory drainage arrangements can be made with a little forethought and examination of other stables near by. The slope of the passageway of the barn should not be more than one inch in eighteen. This is necessary for comfort of the horse's legs and feet and is sufficient to carry away moisture.

If the passageway is not sloped, a drain pipe, with grates, should be installed under the floor before it is put down. A good flooring for the stable is clay. Concrete, stones, bricks, asphalt, wood and cobblestones are also used for stall and stable floors. They are advisable in the order named. However, clay is preferable.

It is best that the stable be roomy and high so that air can circulate without creating a draft. Because sunlight is beneficial to horses, the more windows the better. The stall window should be high enough to prevent the horse from sticking his head out, or his playing with the screen or pane. Horizontal sliding windows are generally preferred to the vertical type in the barn. They are easier to open because of their height.

FIG. 16   A barn with center passageway and box stalls on each side.

Fig. 17   A barn with overhanging passageway.

Light colors inside the barn, contrary to some opinion, will not affect the horse's eyesight. A good suggestion is to place an electric light flush with the ceiling in every stable. The switch should be near the stall door in an inconspicuous spot. One or more fire extinguishers must be easily accessible in all barns.

For the inside of the barn, iron grating over the upper parts of the doors and partitions is recommended in preference to wood. However, if iron grating is used, have it spread so the horse cannot stick his muzzle through the bars. In his book on the different kinds of wood for stable purposes, Hayes says, "A horse is apt to gnaw or start to crib on elm more than any other type of wood."

Tile makes the best roof. It is fireproof, and though more expensive, will last indefinitely.

An inner roof about one foot from the outer one, so that the air will stop the change in temperature from being felt too quickly inside, is advantageous.

The outside doors of the barn should be large enough to minimize chances of accidents and to allow carts, buggies and other necessary stable tack to be easily ushered through. Both for outside doors and those on box stalls, sliding doors are better than the swinging type. The sliding door is safer and out of the way at all times. If sliding doors cannot be used, be certain the doors open outward. Stall doors and stall openings should be at least four feet across. This is particularly necessary for a mare with a foal at foot.

If the barn has stalls on both sides, the center passage should be at least eight feet wide. This will enable you to work effectively on your horse while he is in the cross-ties, and will also leave room for another horse to pass. When in cross-ties, your horse stands in the center passage with ropes fastened from the halter to both sides of the passageway. In this position he is easily groomed. See Figure 18.

Any medicine chests or shelves should be fastened high on the walls to prevent horses rubbing against them.

Now for a word about stalls. The box type is preferable to the tie or narrow standing stall. The horse is always free to move about in a box stall, while he has to be constantly tied with his hind feet in litter in a standing stall. This may bring about lameness, or thrush—to say nothing of the discomfort to the animal.

The minimum size suggested for a box stall is 11 by 11 feet, especially if tail boards are used. These are small boards built out several inches from the wall, completely around the stall. They strike the horse between the hocks and tail in height. This prevents him from rubbing his tail against the walls.

Stalls at Cumberland View Farm, Richmond, Kentucky, home of the famous Saddle Bred sire, *King's Genius* 9500, are at least 16 by 16 feet.

Some breeders and owners believe that partitions between stalls should be closed so a horse may not bother or be bothered by his stablemates. Other owners believe in allowing the horses to see and enjoy each other's company. There are points in favor of both opinions, so the decision rests with the individual. Stallions usually are kept to themselves as they often irritate the other horses in the barn.

The stables, and especially the stalls, should be disinfected at least twice a year with a good disinfectant. If a horse is moved from one stall to another, both stalls should be disinfected before the changes are made.

If your horse is a "kicker," a mat or some other substitute may be hung or fastened to the walls. This will protect both his legs and feet and the stall.

Be sure to use separate receptacles for hay and grain in each stall. If these feeds are in the same manger, the horse will search for the grain before he will touch the hay, throwing the latter aside with impatience.

Iron is the best material for water pails and the manger, and will be more economical because of its durability. Place the water bucket in the corner opposite the manger. It is not good for the animal's digestion to eat and drink at the same time.

For only $6.59 you can buy an automatic cast iron water bowl which will save you a lot of work and give your horse water as he needs it. The device is made so that on lowering his muzzle to drink, he presses a small nose plate inside the bowl. This starts the flow of water. A little water is always left in the bowl and the device is designed not to squirt or overflow.

In our suggestions for the barn, we wish to stress the advantage of separate rooms for feed, tack, cleaning and washing. Saddlery

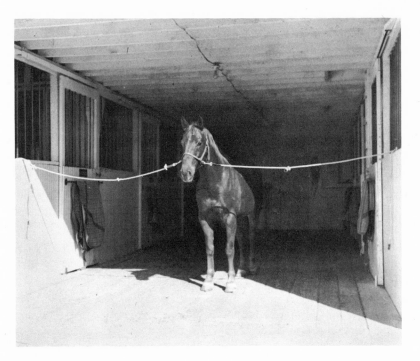

Fig. 18   The above colt is cross-tied in the passageway of the barn.

and harness are referred to as tack. If your space and money are limited, however, plan a combination of the first three. The benefit of separate rooms is to keep dirt and stable odors from the equipment. Well constructed feed bins also discourage rodents. A wash rack for cleaning carts and other tack is an asset.

If several horses are to be stabled together, a "sick" box stall, away from the other stalls, is almost a necessity. Care must be taken to prevent a sick horse from transmitting his ailment to a neighbor. In addition, he should not be permitted to graze near the other horses. There is a great chance of infection if a well horse grazes where a sick horse has been.

The necessary equipment for an up-to-date horseman includes a good broom, sponges, sweat scraper, stable fork, skep or bushel basket, water and wash pails, sieve, measuring cup for grain, hoof pick, body and dandy brushes, wiping and cleaning cloths and rubber curry combs. A wheel barrow is very handy and also fetlock shears, electric clippers, leather punch, leg bandages, leg wash, disinfectant, stable sheet, cooler and blanket for cold weather. If you board your horse in a public stable, nearly all these articles will be provided, with the possible exception of saddlery, horse clothing and tail sets, if they are used. We will explain the use for such equipment later on when we discuss grooming, saddlery and equipment.

After you have owned a horse for some time, you will accumulate many simple and complicated horse medicines and remedies. The fewer of these concoctions you have, the better for your horse. Horses are more often overdosed for illness than underdosed. Many of your horsemen acquaintances will have numerous suggestions to offer regarding the dosing of your horse and unless you are very confident of your friend's knowledge, first consult the veterinarian. Following bad advice in treating even a minor ailment might be very harmful.

Kindness and patience are the keys to successful handling of horses, especially in the stable. Horses are highly strung animals and need gentle treatment. Nearly all so-called "bad" horses are made so by unkind handling of thoughtless persons. It is rare indeed for a horse to act with maliciousness or meanness. Such acts generally are the result of an improperly conveyed command

and misunderstanding by the horse. Even when seriously ill he will not stop fighting back until he drops in his tracks, and in a pulling contest the animal is sure to win over the human. Therefore it is necessary to be able to judge when he is not feeling fit.

The horse is unable to reason and if not given food and careful attention, will often shy for months from anyone or anything that has frightened or injured him. Never punish him except when he commits an offense. Otherwise, he is liable to be confused as to the reason for punishment. He will not recognize being punished for something he has done, unless it is at the time he commits the offense. Also never punish him in anger, but see that he obeys you.

To teach or school your horse in stable manners, a light tap with the whip is enough to let him know he is wrong. A pat on the neck and a kind word should likewise be given for good behavior. The horse does not understand what you say but he does understand the manner and tone of voice that you use. Teach him to be quiet and obedient around the stable.

Regarding bedding in the stalls: in the Northern States straw is most commonly used, and in the South wood shavings are most popular. Both of these are elastic, absorbent and adequate. Peat moss is not used in this country. Shavings are often more economical as they can be had for little more than the price of hauling them away from the sawmill. A stall bedded with them can be more easily cleaned or mucked out than one bedded with straw.

The prime test of good bedding is its elastic and absorbent qualities. If straw is used, wheat is a bit more absorbent than oat. Sawdust or sand should never be considered for bedding material.

All stalls should be mucked out and aired daily, as dung and urine not only will cause a stench and attract insects and vermin, but have a very bad effect on horses' feet. It is best if your horse can be out during the day, but if he has to stay in his stall, try to remove the droppings several times a day.

Arrange to let your horse roll as often as he desires. This is one of the advantages of having large box stalls. Rolling rests and refreshes him. During the summer months you can let him roll during his grazing periods. If you permit him to roll while you have him on a lead, be extremely careful he does not become fouled with the lead strap.

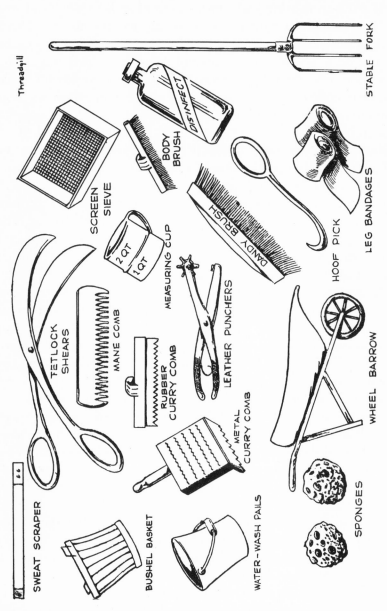

Threadgill

STABLE FORK

BODY BRUSH

SCREEN SIEVE

DISINFECT

LEG BANDAGES

HOOF PICK

DANDY BRUSH

MEASURING CUP

2 QT
1 QT

FETLOCK SHEARS

MANE COMB

LEATHER PUNCHERS

RUBBER CURRY COMB

METAL CURRY COMB

WHEEL BARROW

SWEAT SCRAPER

BUSHEL BASKET

WATER–WASH PAILS

SPONGES

FIG. 19   Equipment needed for grooming, feeding and general care.

A stable keeper sometimes will try to prevent a horse from rolling when outside the barn as he will get dirt and sand in his skin that will take a lot of extra grooming to remove. If you can prevent this practice, you should do so.

Do not allow your horse to be tied in his box stall unless absolutely necessary. If it should become necessary to do so temporarily, because of illness or for some other reason, be sure the tie rope is long enough for him to move his head, but not long enough for him to get his foot over and cause a rope burn or some other trouble. At all times leave the halter off in the stall, especially on young horses.

In the warm summer months, while the horse is in his stall, keep a lightweight cotton sheet on him for protection from flies. Spray the barn and stalls regularly with an effective insecticide.

If your horse rubs against the sides of his stall, posts or tailboards, examine him for ticks or mange. Keep his tail washed and picked out weekly, using soft water. The horse's tail will itch if not properly cared for. Soft water regularly applied to the mane and tail will also stimulate growth.

If he is not eating properly, as the saying goes "is off his feed," examine his back teeth or grinders for rough edges. These teeth sometimes wear, especially on older horses. They become sharp so that the animal cannot masticate properly. When this happens, he will often stop eating and consequently fall off in weight. If after examination you find the edges of his teeth are rough, call a veterinarian immediately and have him attend to them.

We hope our suggestions on stable management will assist you in having a clean, well-managed stable that you can be proud of.

CHAPTER V

Feeding

The most important rules of feeding a horse are regularity and frequency. Though three feedings per day are customary, five feedings spaced between the hours of 5:00 A.M. and 11:00 P.M. are better for the animal. The stomach of the horse is small. This makes frequent feedings more desirable than in the case of some other animals. The quantity of feed for the day should be divided by the number of times fed. Horses that have been worked hard during the day should be given a bit heavier feeding at night.

If you are caring for your own horse, it may not be possible for you to feed him three times a day. In such case, leave some hay in the stall before him throughout the day. Or, if he has a pasture, turn him out after his morning feed.

It is best to give him a little hay before any grain is given. This takes the edge off the horse's appetite and will stop him from "bolting" his grain. Some owners feed "chop," which is hay cut in lengths of about an inch, mixed in with the grain. Chops, like salt bricks in the manger, also discourages the "bolting" of grain. Many breeders recommend that hay be left in the stall at all times.

All horses do not require the same amount of hay or grain. The amount given to each must be based on his individual requirements, which must be closely watched. If you have an Arab or a Quarter Horse, your grain requirements may be less than with some other breeds.

For your information, the following is the amount of daily feed recommended by the United States Cavalry for light horses under 1,150 pounds that are in good condition. The Cavalry has been unusually successful in caring for its horses. It has arrived at this table through much experimentation:

10 lbs. Oats		8 lbs. Oats
14 lbs. Hay	or	5 lbs. Alfalfa
		9 lbs. Other Type Hay

or
6 lbs. Oats
2 lbs. Corn
5 lbs. Alfalfa
9 lbs. Other Type Hay

If the horse does not eat all the grain given him at a feeding, his grain ration should be reduced accordingly. The quantity of feed given the horse should be based upon the amount of work he has to do. If the animal is doing a little work, has been sick, or on a long lay-off, he should receive a proportionate quantity of food and laxative.

Underfeeding and lack of appetite can often be remedied by changing the ration, adding a little ginger or fresh vegetables, and paying careful attention to the proper amount of exercise. Not all feed eaten is digested. One should note the undigested expenditure on the part of the digestive organs. Too much feed of this kind is undesirable.

In changing diets, do so gradually. If it is necessary to alter the grain ration, as from oats to corn, the oat rations should be cut in half and the new feed steadily increased, so that the animal will become accustomed to the change. If the corn and oats are fed together, the corn should be ground or cracked, as corn is harder than oats to digest. Corn also seems to generate heat and it is not considered as good a grain as oats for feeding in desert areas.

Work and exercise should be avoided directly after feeding, as the stomach and bowels are then distended and any pressure against the lungs will cause distress and interfere with digestion. Exercise directly after feeding will cause a looseness of the bowels. The feed remains in the stomach about one and one-half hours. Until this time has elapsed, exercise should be deferred. Quietness around the barns while the horse is feeding is also conducive to good digestion.

Likewise, you should not feed your horse immediately after any strenuous exercise. A little hay is all right, but he should not have his grain for at least an hour. The horse must always be watered before, not after, feeding. Until he is cooled out after strenuous exercise, give him only a few swallows.

All of the forage for the horse should be wholesome, clean,

well prepared and given at regular intervals for the sake of economy. Before feeding hay, it should be shaken out with a fork to get rid of the dust and seed. Wheat or rye chaff should not be used as a feed as it often gets lodged in the throat. This makes it necessary to screen grain to eliminate the dust, dirt and other small particles of foreign matter. The screening should be done just prior to feeding and can be done with specially manufactured measuring cups, which have a fine screen made into the bottom.

Crushed or rolled oats are easier to digest than whole oats and consequently are more economical for there is little waste. If barley is used as a feed, it must always be crushed. Its husk is too hard to digest.

A bran mash ought to be given each horse at least twice a week, if dry bran is not given daily mixed in with the grain. The mash may be prepared for the average horse by pouring boiling water over three pounds of bran. Use enough water to wet the bran thoroughly and add an ounce of salt. Then cover and allow it to steam for an hour or more. In England bran mashes are the custom every Saturday night.

As salt is very necessary to the health of the horse, salt or a salt brick should be in every stall so the horse can lick it as he wants it. One or two chunks of salt in the horse's manger will be handy for him.

It is natural for the horse to feed off the ground. This makes the saliva glands function better, thereby aiding mastication. Hay is often fed from racks as high as the animal's head, or even higher, but we still suggest feeding off the ground. In this way there is little danger of a seed or any other minute particle falling into his eye and causing irritation.

During the summer months, if you are not turning your horse into a pasture for the day, he should be taken out on a lead and permitted to graze for one-half hour or more daily. In the winter, when grazing in some parts of the country is impossible, chopped carrots are an excellent substitute for green grass.

Proper watering of a horse is just as important as proper feeding. A horse will drink from five to fifteen gallons of water daily. In the winter time or during the colder months, the amount will decrease slightly. If a horse has water before him constantly, he will never drink to excess, so the practice of giving each horse his own water bucket or automatic bowl in his stall is highly recommended. The water given must always be clean and pure and in a clean receptacle.

A horse should be watered at least three times a day and at regular periods. If the water is very cold, as it sometimes is from a deep well, it is best to let it stand for a while to take off the chill.

It is very important that water pails, troughs and mangers be kept clean. The pails should be scrubbed daily with wet sand or some other cleanser, rinsed thoroughly and dried in the sun. The mangers should be brushed out daily with a stiff brush and at least once a week scraped and washed with soap and water. If daily cleaning requires more time than you have, you should strive to clean them as often as possible as this will help to keep your horse well and healthy.

The object of food, water and air is to furnish material for repair of body waste and heat. We will not go into the chemical analysis of the different feeds, but we will divide them into three classifications:

1. Nitrogenous matter (fat, starch and sugar).
2. Water and mineral salts.
3. Fibre, which aids in digestion but does not supply energy.

Some foods produce muscle, others energy, while still others produce fat. According to Hayes in his book on stable management, hay, even when carefully stored, suffers continued nutritive loss from chemical changes going on within it. He states that new hay, even in February, is superior to hay a year older. It is known that when horses are deprived of all food except water, the thin ones will live from five to ten days and those in good condition will live from three to five weeks. Twelve or thirteen days is the longest a horse will survive without food or water. Sugar in water is the best way to revive a horse that is dying from hunger.

In mentioning the qualities of the various feeds, we will begin with the most popular—oats. Oats are far superior to any other type of grain for horse feeding purposes. The shape and weight of oats will vary averaging around thirty-five to forty-five pounds to the bushel. Oats that are of good quality should be clean, have a pleasing odor, feel dry, be hard and elastic, and full of flour with a thin husk. If they fill these requirements, they are old enough to feed, contain sufficient nutriment and have not been subjected to dampness. Shriveled or dusty oats are inferior, and oats that are too new usually act as a laxative and are not as digestible as those a year old.

Corn comes next to oats in food value. As it is hard, it is best to have it cracked or ground for feeding. If ground, we suggest grinding the cob with it. The cob is rich in woody fibre and about one-fifth the weight of well dried corn is cob. If the cob cannot be used, the corn should be crushed or cracked and mixed with bran or "chop." It takes a horse about fifteen minutes to eat one pound of hay and five to ten minutes to eat one pound of corn.

Carefully stored corn will retain its vitality for many years. The dryer the grain, the more readily will the digestive juices penetrate it, thus making digestion much easier. One year is sufficient time for drying corn.

We will not mention the relative merits of barley, wheat, peas or beans as horse feeds, for they are seldom used in private or public stables in this country today. They are all much inferior to oats or corn.

Bran should be fed in conjunction with other feeds, or as mentioned, as bran mash at least once a week. If the bran is not fed, the horse should have a supply of chopped, fresh carrots daily to take its place.

A handful of linseed meal mixed in the regular grain ration and used once a day is a good tonic. It will also help to give a good coat. However, do not expect linseed meal to take the place of good grooming.

There are several conditioners and tonics on the market and we have noticed that many breeders and trainers have their own concoctions. They mix these themselves the same as they do leg-washes and cold remedies. We recall one of these tonics, which was a conditioner made by Mr. and Mrs. Seymour Boardman of Miami, Florida. This mixture was one-half bone meal and one-half crushed oyster shells.

All of the Boardman horses got one tablespoon a day in the noon feed. There are many such combinations and we have known many trainers who use about two to four pounds of barley meal mixed in with the regular feed ration to condition and fatten horses. However, we do not recommend that any tonic be given except on the advice of a veterinarian.

Straw, as a feed, has little nutritive value except where the horse is on corn. At this time it will appeal to the horse's appetite, if given in a chopped state. When the corn ration is decreased, the straw "chop" should be discontinued.

Hay should be considered as grass when studying its feeding qualities, for there are many varieties of grass from which it can be made. Those most commonly fed in this country are alfalfa, timothy, clover and lespedeza. Perhaps we should include peanut, pea and Johnson grass, but we are not recommending that they be used as horse feeds.

Johnson grass hay is widely fed through the Black Belt, and Tennessee Walking Horse country in Alabama. Peanut hay is also fed in the Southeast as both hays are grown locally.

The benefits of the different types of hay are often disputed, but we believe that for any horse in good condition, timothy is the best. For a horse in need of conditioning, alfalfa, lespedeza or a mixture of hay containing alfalfa is better. Alfalfa by itself acts too much as a laxative. Some horsemen feed alfalfa as a meal, but this is not generally recommended.

Many breeders and trainers believe in keeping hay in front of their horses at all times. With some horses this would prove quite expensive, as they would scatter feed from one end of the stall to the other. All horses should be made to clean up their hay and if they fail to do so, the amount given should be reduced. We witnessed the feeding of a colt that would take time to pull his hay out of the manger, scatter it about his stall and then drop down and eat it.

Grandeau and Leclerc have shown that an average horse will maintain his weight on seventeen and one-half pounds of hay, or on five pounds of oats and five pounds of hay per day. It is also well known that a horse turned out to pasture can keep in good health, but his muscular powers will decrease with his lower feeding requirements. Therefore, if you want your horse to keep in good condition when you turn him out to pasture, it is best to also feed him about five pounds of oats or corn daily. Some owners put a horse in pasture for a month or more of rest and then recondition him.

A suggested ration for healthy, light horses getting little or no exercise is:

3 lbs. Oats*		4 lbs. Oats
17 lbs. Hay	or	13 lbs. Hay
5 lbs. Bran		2½ lbs. Bran
Handful of linseed meal		7 lbs. Carrots.

Ration for light horses with small amount of exercise:

        7 lbs. Oats
        17 lbs. Hay
        3 lbs. Bran
        3 lbs. Carrots.

Ration for light horses being worked daily:

        14 lbs. Oats
        13 lbs. Hay
        3 lbs. Bran
        3 lbs. Carrots.

Naturally, this diet will not fit all horses. The amount and type of exercise would cause the diet to be varied. However, it can be used as a guide.

Commercial feeds may be used and often are mixed with molasses. The analysis of the feed will be printed on the sack as well as the proportions to feed. You can judge from the analysis whether you will want to use it. Molasses is a good appetizer and is also a carbohydrate food. A quart a day with two parts of water can be mixed with grain or roughage.

When feeding a mare in foal one of the most important requirements is good grass, carrots and plenty of salt and water. Mares are generally bred in the spring and during the summer months, extending from April to about October, they should not be given corn.

* A pound of oats is equivalent to a quart of grain. Corn and barley are heavier grains and if they are fed, a quart will weigh more than a pound.

A suggested ration up to October is:

> 3 qts. Oats
> 1 qt. Bran (given morning and evening,
> as a mare in foal should only be fed
> twice a day)

After October:

> 2 qts. Oats
> 1 qt. Cracked Corn
> 1 qt. Bran.

After the foal is born, it will eat from the dam's feed box, so substitute rolled or crushed oats and plenty of hay and water. When the foal reaches six weeks or more, let him have his own feed box and also, if possible, skim milk and lime water every day. From six weeks until the colt is weaned, give the mare four quarts of grain a day in two feedings. After the weaning, feed her three times daily. After six months, the foal can be fed six quarts of grain daily and at ten months, seven quarts daily. When he reaches fifteen months, raise the ration to eight quarts of grain but do not forget the carrots.

These are general feeding suggestions but circumstances arise when your own judgment must be used.

CHAPTER VI

Grooming, Shoeing and Veterinary Remedies

Grooming

Grooming, or cleaning your horse's skin by friction and massage is as essential to his health and well-being as it is to his appearance. It removes the particles of dust, dirt and dried sweat which otherwise would clog the free action of oil and sweat glands. Rubbing also removes scurf which is no longer needed on the surface of the skin. The glossy, sleek coat that appears is not only due to the absence of dirt and polishing of the hair, but also to the increased secretion from oil glands in the skin. This oil is drawn out by massage and thorough grooming.

Ideally, your horse should be groomed in the morning to remove the excretions of the pores which have formed during the night. If you are caring for your own horse, however, and are busy during the day, you may have to groom him before putting him up at night and after you have ridden or exercised him. A horse that has not been exercised during the day will require more grooming than one that has been exercised and cleaned immediately thereafter. This is due to his sweating and the pores being open. Rubbing will more effectively clean the skin when the pores are open than if delayed until they are closed and perspiration has had a chance to dry and cake.

When your horse is heated, you should never permit him to stand unattended longer than necessary. Hand rubbing is the best way to dry him. It is better than cooling him out with a woolen cooler (blanket). However, in cold weather, unless you have someone to work quickly with you on the animal, the "cooler" method is better. It will prevent him from catching cold. Even then part of the cooler may be turned back to enable you to rub a small area.

Do not attempt to brush your horse if he is still wet. Have him rubbed thoroughly and "cooled out" before starting the brushing.

There is more than one way to cool out a wet horse. If it is not too cold or drafty, go over him with a sweat scraper, then take a linen cloth about a yard square, or a clean piece of burlap, and rub him briskly until dry. Then go over him with a dandy brush to smooth out the hairs. If the "cooler" method is used, be sure to cover the animal immediately from head to tail. Then walk him dry in a spot where there is no draft. When the horse is thoroughly dry, he may be brushed.

Many horsemen will not take enough pains to wrap the legs and walk their horse, but are content to throw the "cooler" over him and let him stand in cross-ties or in his stall. Sooner or later this will cause trouble. During the summer months there may be only "scratches" (sneezes) but in the colder months, the horse is apt to come down with a serious cold. In any event, let us emphasize—never "put up" your horse until he is dry.

As we have stated, there is more to grooming than just removing the superficial dirt and straightening the coat. To correctly groom your horse, it is necessary that you go all over him briskly, using circular strokes. Use a rubber curry comb. The only time it is permissible to use a metal curry comb is in spring when his coat is longer or if he has rolled in clay or mud and it has dried on him. Even in these cases use the metal curry comb very gently on your horse's body. If he is well blanketed during winter, his coat is not apt to thicken so much. The main use for your curry comb is to clean hair and dirt out of your dandy brush.

After you have gone over your horse with the rubber or metal curry comb, then go over him vigorously with the dandy brush. Start at his head, on his left side (near side) and work back. Be sure not to forget his legs. He will enjoy being rubbed and brushed. Though customarily you put him in cross-ties while grooming, a well mannered horse will stand quietly without being tied.

If you have time, after finishing with the dandy brush, a good hand rubbing, using a "whisp" of straw, will make your horse feel like a "million." To bring out a sheen after this workout, you might go over him with a cloth or short haired body brush, being sure to place emphasis on his legs.

We do not recommend the use of a rag or sawdust which has

been moistened with coal oil, kerosene or any other flammable oil for rubbing into the horse's hide to make him shine or take out the dandruff. If he is on the proper diet and has the right and regular amount of grooming, this is never necessary. At horse shows, especially at night events, rubbing a little vaseline or olive oil on your hands and going over the horse's body so that he will shine under the lights is excusable. However, you will find that the oil will pick up a lot of dirt that you will have to brush out.

Now take a small damp sponge and wash out your horse's eyes, nostrils and dock. Whenever necessary, clean out the sheath of a stallion or gelding with warm soapy water.

If your horse is a five-gaited American Saddle Bred, Tennessee Walker, Morgan, pony or any other breed which carries a full mane and tail, never put a comb through them. It will break and pull out the hairs. Brush his mane, forelock and tail lightly and pick them out by starting at the bottom of the hairs and generally working upward to untangle and straighten them. You may wash the mane and tail. If you do so, allow them to dry and then pick them out with your fingers. The mane of the three-gaited horse is cut right down to his neck and the hairs of the tail shaved down to the dock. Your care of the tail is obviously different in this case.

If your horse is a Thoroughbred hunter or jumper, you will want to keep his mane and tail thinned. You can do so by pulling out a few hairs at a time. The roots of the mane and tail are tough and it does not hurt the horse. Begin on the underside and pull the longer hairs first until the mane is well thinned and about four inches long. The tail is thinned by pulling the long stiff hairs along the dock and the bushy part of his tail. You can shorten his tail by merely pulling the longer hairs out. You may also use thinning scissors and cut it to the length you want.

After you have cleaned and brushed your horse, use a hoof pick to clean out the foreign matter in each hoof. Notice if there is a foul odor. If so, it may be a symptom of thrush or a rotting of the hoof, and you can begin to treat it. At the time of grooming, also notice any swelling or lameness and then doctor any minor ailments you know how to take care of. Should you notice anything you do not fully understand, call your veterinarian.

During hot weather, your horse may sometimes "break out" (start to sweat) while in the barn. If this should happen, bring him out of the stall and rub him down. See that he has plenty of fresh water and check his feed to be sure that he is not on too rich a diet. If he continues to sweat profusely, call your veterinarian as it might be serious.

You will note that at no time have we advocated washing or using any water whatsoever on your horse's body, with the exception of his eyes, nostrils, mane and tail.

In the spring many horse owners have their horses clipped or partially clipped. Nature, however, gives him two new coats a year and the old coat may be hurried on its way by good grooming. Some say that his coat never looks the same after it has once been clipped. We believe that if you diligently groom your horse and blanket him during the colder months, you will not find it necessary to have him clipped—not all over anyway. However, if you do have him clipped all over, be sure to keep him covered until he has had a chance to acclimate himself to the change.

As a horse owner, you should take great pride in your horse's appearance. Keep his ears trimmed out, the long hairs off the fetlock joints and the hair from protruding over the coronary band down onto the hoof. Also cut the long hairs around his eyes and muzzle. The hairs around his muzzle act as feelers when he is feeding, but in the stable your horse need not forage unnecessarily for his food.

This method of grooming, as we have outlined, will take the greater part of an hour, including "picking out the feet." We appreciate the fact that not all horses are as thoroughly cleaned as we recommend and many are even better cared for. You will have to work within your own time limitations, but we feel sure that if you do understand these fundamentals of grooming, you will do a better job and be proud of your horse.

In the stall he cannot move about as he can when in pasture, and with the grooming and clipping, his coat does not offer the protection that it would with the dandruff and scurf in it before grooming. To take the place of these natural benefits, we give the horse a balanced diet, a softer bed and in winter a sheet or blanket to keep him warm.

Shoeing

If you are fortunate enough to have near-by a competent shoer of the breed of horse you own, he can be of invaluable service to you. If there is none in your area, you will have to use the best farrier available and seek the advice of another horseman on shoeing problems. Shoes affect your horse's way of going and may be specially built and weighted to aid or improve his movements or correct his faults.

In any case, be very sure your farrier is competent before you experiment with your horse's feet. Faulty shoeing can be the cause of many foot ailments and a careless and ignorant blacksmith may inflict damage to healthy feet. It is best that the farrier "make the shoe fit the hoof" rather than the "hoof to fit the shoe."

Your horse should be shod at least once a month as his hoof may grow more than one-half inch in that period. If new shoes are not needed, the old ones may be re-set and the hoof pared down where necessary. If your horse has been turned to pasture for a rest period, you may want to pull off his shoes, but in that case, too, his feet must be regularly attended to or rasped down.

If you have a pleasure horse that you ride generally on weekends and not over hard, stony country, you can perhaps safely let your horse go unshod to save the expense of regular shoeing. However, you must keep his feet checked as they may become sore.

Shoeing is fairly expensive. For Saddle Bred show horses that carry a long toe and weighted shoes to get action, it will run about $24.00. Shoeing a Western type horse will only cost about $12.00. However, if you are using your Saddle Bred as a hack in cross-country riding, his feet may be kept short like a hunter's or the Western type horse, and he is shod similarly.

"Interfering" and "brushing," meaning striking of the striding foot against another, is sometimes caused by bad shoeing. On the other hand, these same faults and others, such as "winging," which is a paddling-like stride, or "going wide behind," may be remedied by careful shoeing. If you have cause to believe that your horse's shoes are not well fitted, one test is to remove the shoes for five or six days in order that the wearing parts of the hoof may show the type shoe that will fit. Different horses have to be shod differently.

Horses nowadays do not have as much foot trouble as they used to because of the use of pads and various foot dressings which protect the feet and keep them healthy. Lanolin and lamb's cotton are good when used with leather foot pads. These pads cover the feet and protect them from stones and foreign matter. Pads are not commonly used in desert areas, however, due to heat.

In shoeing the hunter and jumper, special care must be taken that the frog (horny cushion of the foot) rests well on the ground to cushion the foot and absorb the shock in jumping. Hunters and jumpers are often shod with special shoes to keep them from slipping. Calks or small pieces of metal on the bottom of the shoe dig into the ground and prevent slipping.

Care of the feet and shoeing is an inexhaustible subject and experienced horsemen give it every consideration.

Followers of the various breeds of horses always claim their own breed needs the most careful shoeing. They are all justified in their opinions. Naturally, racing horses and draft animals must have the proper shoe carefully fitted or they could not perform their respective jobs efficiently. Equally important are the shoes of the Saddle Bred, Tennessee Walker, Arab, the hunter, jumper or whatever breed or type you own. Much of the Saddle Bred's action and way of going depends not only on the weight and shape of the shoes but also on the amount of toe and heel he carries. The angle the toe and heel make with the ground differs. Forty-five degrees for the toe and fifty-five degrees for the heel is ideal and the blacksmith should measure these angles and not guess at them. The toe also runs about four and three-quarter inches in length, and should be measured. Not every horse will carry these exact measurements and they must be adjusted to his way of going.

The angles of measurement applicable to hunters and jumpers are the measurements of the toes of the forefeet and hindfeet. They generally run fifty in front and fifty-three behind. The Western type generally carries fifty-one in front and fifty-four or fifty-five behind. These angles too, depend on the horse and fit the way of going of a particular horse.

The Tennessee Walker for show also may have special weighting devices and heavy shoes to give desired action and overstride. The shoe may weigh up to two pounds; some are even heavier. In any case, the farrier must study your horse and may have to experiment to find what he needs to improve his way of going.

Just any "shoer" cannot properly shoe your horse. However, most blacksmiths can do what you tell them, provided you know WHAT to tell them.

It is impossible for anyone to donate advice on the horse's way of going unless that person has actually seen the horse in his gaits. To counteract any faults in your horse's way of going, and at all times when it comes to horse shoes, we suggest that you seek the services of the best shoer of the breed or type of horse you have in your community. If you have none available and do not have faith in the blacksmith in your vicinity, seek the advice of a trainer.

We have made no attempt to recommend any specific type of shoe, nor have we tried to tell you how to make or fit them, for we believe shoeing is a skilled profession that requires many years of experience to achieve proficiency. However, we want to impress upon you as an amateur the importance of proper shoeing and obtaining the advice and services of persons who are experienced in handling your type animal.

Common Ailments and Veterinary Remedies

Sooner or later, at shows or wherever horsemen congregate, you will overhear or enter into controversies concerning the merits or demerits of various simple veterinary remedies for your horse. These discussions are often comical and differences of opinion usually wax hottest over cold remedies or something "guaranteed" to grow hair. For instance, over a small "saddle gall," one will vow "bacon fat will grow the same color hair on that spot in three days," whereas another will say: "No, sir, it won't! Nothing will grow hair on that spot but vaseline." In all probability the hair would grow in the same color without anything being applied. Most anything at all will help; but the point is that the men came from different localities and they have their own specific home remedies for minor ailments, which they swear by. Consequently, there are many "sure cures" for the same ailments, each one just about as good as the other. We have listened to a great many of these correctives—from packing a barb-wire cut with lime to amputating a leg. Good stories are a traditional part of every sport and horsemen can rival fishermen for the one that "got away" and it all makes good listening.

The ailments and remedies discussed here are some of the more common ones that may affect your horse. But again we say that unless you are absolutely certain of your diagnosis, seek the advice of a veterinarian. You might treat and dose for the wrong ailment and consequently do more harm than good.

Dr. J. Lee Hopkins, veterinary surgeon of Atlanta, Georgia, related an incident once in which a horseman from North Georgia was purging his favorite gelding for worms and nearly killed the horse. The gelding kept falling off in weight and his condition worsened, until it was discovered that an altogether different treatment was necessary. You too, can make the same mistake. The following are some ailments compiled from our observation, from breeders, doctors and books, along with the general treatment for them which we hope will be helpful to you.

ACUTE INDIGESTION: This is very serious and is caused by over-eating and over-loading the stomach. Your horse will become stiff, breathe hard and sweat profusely. Call a veterinarian immediately. If you cannot locate your veterinarian, give the horse a laxative and then rub his stomach vigorously with hot towels. Also give injections of warm, soapy water.

ANASARCA: (Swollen legs.) This is more common in the hind legs than in the front. It is generally caused by a diet that is too rich. It will often cause the sheath to swell in stallions or geldings and the teats to swell in mares. The swelling will often go down overnight and then come up again the next day. In treating anasarca, it is best to eliminate corn, feed less oats and increase the bran ration. A laxative is recommended with the change of feed.

CONSTIPATION: Increase his bran ration and let him have green grass or a quart or more of chopped carrots daily. Be sure that your horse drinks plenty of fresh, clean water.

CRIBBING: In most cases a horse starts cribbing or chewing on wood because he does not get enough exercise. However, it is sometimes caused by the teeth being too close together and the veterinarian can correct this. Cribbing is definitely very hard to stop and a complete cure is almost an impossibility. To stop your horse from cribbing in his stall, remove all objects on which he might be able to crib. If this fails, try buckling a leather strap, about one and one-half to two inches wide, tightly around the upper part of the neck. This strap, if kept tight, will tend to keep the horse from swallowing air and should discourage him from cribbing.

Electricity will do the job, if these remedies fail, but only an electrical serviceman should install the wiring. A horse cannot withstand the amount of electrical shock that a human can so extreme care must be taken. The ideal outfit is one of the electrical fence transformers that are on the market for approximately $20.00. Piano wire can be effectively used by stringing it along the tail boards and places where the horse has a tendency to crib.

POLL EVIL, FISTULA, THISTELO AND SADDLE GALLS: These are various names for sore spots occurring on different parts of the horse from his poll (the top of his head) to his withers. They are caused by bruising, generally from a bad fitting saddle or a tight bridle. There will be swelling which often contains pus. Some cases will have to be lanced by a veterinarian before the sore spot will heal.

COLDS, SHIPPING FEVER AND DISTEMPER: These conditions may develop from many causes such as seasonal changes, shipping from one place to another or "cooling out" in a draft. These ailments are contagious and one horse can pass them to another. Treat such cases by placing the horse in a large, light, airy stall that is free from drafts. Have the stall well bedded with fresh, clean straw. Bandage the horse's legs after having rubbed them with a good leg wash.

There are many good cough medicines on the market, should your horse have a cough. You can make your own mixture of pine tar and kerosene or honey which is good. Should the glands under the jaw or his neck be swollen, rub them with camphorated oil twice daily. It may be necessary to have the glands lanced, if the swelling does not go down.

Be sure to isolate a horse with a cold. Do not allow him to graze in spots where other horses are grazing.

WORMS: There are several types of worms that may afflict horses and the wrong medicine might cause more harm than good. It is best to call a veterinarian and have him make a microscopic examination of the dung. This is the only sure way of prescribing the correct treatment. Worms may be found in the horse's droppings or under his tail. It is important that treatment for worms be started immediately as they will quickly put your horse in bad condition. Dr. George H. Conn, noted veterinarian, recommends a phenothiazene mixture on feeds for a period of three weeks to discourage all parasites.

LAMENESS: There are many conditions of the legs and feet which may cause your horse to be lame, or may cause unsightly blemishes. Leg ailments are generally maladies of the bones, ligaments or tendons. To locate lameness, look over your horse carefully while he is resting in his stall, have him move over and notice if he steps over or if he hops. If he hops with a hind leg, then check the hock for a bone spavin.

BONE SPAVIN is a disease in which the bones of the hock joint become uneven or enlarged and there is swelling and inflammation. The Savoss Medicine Company claims good results with their medicine and they guarantee that they can halt the lameness but cannot always reduce the bony growth that occurs. "Firing" or "blistering" is often resorted to but cannot be guaranteed.

To definitely check for a bone spavin, have another person hold your horse's head while you lift up his fetlock (ankle) close to his stifle bone and hold it there for about two minutes. Now release the leg you were holding and have your assistant "trot out" with the horse. If there is a spavin, the horse will favor the leg.

A good way to check for any lameness is to have the horse trotted on hard ground with only a halter and lead strap, while you stand back and watch. Have the person leading him turn him while at the trot. In this way you will be able to tell just where your horse is lame, as it will hurt him to turn at a trot on a hard surface.

Horses often rest their hind feet on their toes, but should your horse do this with his front feet, there is probably something wrong. With a shoulder lameness, he will generally rest on his toe. If he backs up with difficulty or much effort, check him for shoulder, hip or stifle lameness, or spavin. Also to check for lameness of the shoulder, trot your horse in the same way we mentioned above, but in this case trot him on soft ground.

Any inflammations and splints in your horse's legs can be discovered by running your fingers up and down his legs to feel any fevered spots. Increased temperature in one leg can be detected by feeling the amount of heat in both legs.

SPLINT is a defect or enlargement of the bone between the knee and fetlock. It is so named because of the splint bones that run from the knee to the fetlock joint. Generally it occurs on the inside of the main cannon bone but can also occur on the inside, or outside, of all four legs. "Blistering" will sometimes remove a splint but it is best to diligently use a good medicine. It isn't apt to cause permanent lameness but may cause temporary lameness during its formative stages.

BOG SPAVIN is another condition that attacks the hock. It is caused by an over supply of the fluid that lubricates the hock and forces the ligaments to puff out. It is usually precipitated by strain in over-driving, a fall or injury. There are medicines on the market that will relieve this ailment.

A similar condition that occurs between the tendons and the joints around the ankle is called a WIND-PUFF. As in bog spavin, it is caused by too much secretion of fluid from the glands which results in swellings and puffs. It, too, is caused by straining or over-driving and the treatment is the same as for bog spavin. Both of these conditions are more unsightly than dangerous.

THOROUGHPIN is also practically the same thing as bog spavin, as it is a soft enlargement in the hollow of either side of the hock, but is more serious because of its location. Treatment is the same as for bog spavin.

We might mention that the principal function of the ligaments is to bind the bones together. Damage to the suspensory ligaments of the legs generally occurs from sprain and will probably prevent your horse from doing anything but light work. The tendons are continuations of muscles, and the important ones are in the limbs. Muscles produce heat and perform work, acting voluntarily or involuntarily. Consequently any maladies of the ligaments, tendons and bony structures of the limbs need careful attention to keep your horse from becoming lame and useless to you.

One of the common tendon difficulties that may cause lameness is a bowed tendon. This is a swelling of the tendon between the knee and fetlock joint, and is accompanied by temperature in that locality. Other tendon ailments causing lameness are filled, ruptured, thickened or contracted tendons. Immediate attention in the treatment of these ailments often gets permanent relief. There are many remedies on the market for lameness.

CURB is a swelling of the tendon just below the back of the hock which often is caused by straining, such as rearing or backing too heavy a load while hitched. This swelling sometimes can be seen but, in most cases, it can only be detected by feeling. You must keep in mind that this is a swelling of the tendon and not of the bone. There will be heat through the hock and lameness will result. There are patent medicines on the market that will relieve a curb.

CAPPED HOCK: This is a swelling of the upper part of the hock bone and is usually the result of rubbing or a bruise. Lying on a hard surface may cause it and it can usually be reduced by constant application of a penetrating medicine.

AILMENTS OF THE FEET: There are many ailments of the feet such as thrush, founder, corns, contracted heels and navicular disease. Let us again emphasize great care in cleaning your horse's feet and careful shoeing to prevent disease. The foot of the horse is one of the most important parts of the animal and what has often been said is very true, "No foot—no horse." Care is paramount, for a horse's feet are subject to so many injuries and diseases.

The hoof is the horny box enclosing the elastic and sensitive structures of the foot. It is divided into the wall, sole and frog. The walls and bars of the hoof support the horse's weight. The horn of the wall is the protective covering, similar to one's toe nail. The horny covering grows about one-half inch a month at the heel and toe from the coronary band. The old horn of the sole and frog flakes off as the new grows out. The frog is the triangular mass of horny pad between the bars and sole that protects the sensitive structures above, serving as a cushion to absorb shock and to prevent the feet from slipping.

THRUSH is one of the most common ailments to attack the feet and is a disease generally caused by dirty stalls or barns. The soles, and especially the frogs of the feet, get soft and give off a foul odor. To treat thrush, clean out the hoof, cut away the rotten parts and wash thoroughly with a disinfectant. Then pack the crevices with calomel every day. At the end of three or four days, if you have not noticed a marked improvement, try powdered bluestone. This will surely do the trick. It is absolutely necessary to clean or pick out your horse's feet daily if he is kept in the stable.

CONTRACTED HEELS are caused by ill fitting shoes, which in most cases have remained on the horse's feet too long. As the horn has grown, there has been no part of the foot to give but the soft heels which have had to contract or draw inward.

NAVICULAR DISEASE is an inflammation deep in the hoof and is most often the result of stone bruises. If you live in rocky country, you have to be careful of this. Pads are often worn for protection.

FOUNDER (LAMINITIS) is an inflammation of the sensitive structure of the hoof, in which the sole appears to sag and lose its shape. It does permanent damage to the foot and new growth of the horn almost ceases.

CHAPTER VII

Equipment and Care of Saddlery

Every horse should have his own saddle, bridle and halter. Some people say this is not practical and too expensive, but the United States Cavalry and many other stables provide each animal with his own equipment.

The importance of a well fitting saddle and bridle cannot be overestimated. If every horse could have them individually fitted to him, it would be ideal. However, this is not always possible. The conformation of a horse's back and the type mouth he has will vary. You must be careful that your horse does not develop a sore back because of an ill-fitting saddle, or a sore mouth from a bit that it too harsh.

It will pay you to buy good saddlery, mainly because of its lasting qualities. But just because a saddle is expensive or imported does not necessarily mean that it will fit your horse comfortably. If he has high withers, he should not wear a saddle that would fit a horse with short, thick withers. A properly fitting saddle will render the rider a better seat, and, of course, the best way to check this is to sit in the saddle.

Make sure the front arch of the saddle is not too narrow, for this will pinch the withers and hamper movements of your horse's shoulder muscles. The front arch must not press down nor against the withers. In addition, the spine must be free from pressure.

When a saddle becomes old, or begins to show too much wear, the tree breaks or spreads. If this happens, the saddle should be repaired at once, for that will cause your weight to press down against the withers, spine, or both and cause your horse great discomfort.

A few years ago, hand shaped wood trees were used exclusively in saddles, but now many saddles are fabricated with a metal tree. The former are more likely to break while the latter will bend if

97

given too much usage. Whenever you put your saddle down, place it with the seat down to protect the tree from strain.

Opinion differs as to the relative qualities of imported and domestic saddlery. We believe that American saddle makers are as good as those abroad. In the present market $80.00 will purchase a fine show or other type domestic flat saddle from a reputable dealer. Some can be bought for as little as $35.00, including stirrup leathers and irons. If money is no obstacle, the best quality imported English show saddles can be had for $250.00. The quality and workmanship of these saddles are excellent. They are artistically and skillfully made to show your horse to his best advantage.

Although there are different types and variations of saddles for the different seats in riding, we shall be concerned here with only those generally used.

For pleasure on the bridle path or for show, we suggest the show type English flat saddle, made with a cut back front, because it can be used on several horses. Flat saddles are shaped with enough spread and light padding to fit snug to the back. The seat is flat with only the slightest slope between the pommel (front) and cantle (back). The flaps and skirt are cut straight down on the front to show off your horse's shoulders. The panels, which lie underneath and next to the horse, may be calf-lined and felt-filled. If you have padding on the panels of your saddle, no more padding than is absolutely necessary should be used.

These same saddles can be purchased with a rubber covering on the panels which prevents the saddle from working itself forward on the withers. Many manufacturers will not charge extra for this if requested when ordering the saddle.

Hunting saddles are a type of flat saddle that have a deeper seat set slightly forward. Seats are usually of pigskin. The stirrups are shorter and the flaps more toward the front to permit your legs to rest against them. Concealed under them are knee rolls to brace your knees in jumping. The rolls are made of horse hair covered with leather.

A relatively new type of jumping saddle has been evolved by the Italians. It is the forward seat saddle and is characterized by a more extreme forward seat. It may also have a deeper seat. The

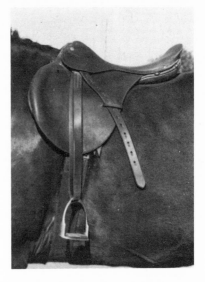

A. English flat saddle, show type.   B. Forward seat saddle.

C. Hunting or polo saddle.   D. Western saddle.

FIG. 20 Types of Saddles.

flaps are well forward and a firm knee roll braces your knees. The panels are stuffed very full in front to form extra support for the knee roll. This seat allows you to lean so far forward, and use such short stirrups, that knee support must be very secure to keep your balance and grip in going over jumps.

The McClellan saddle has been used extensively by the Cavalry. It is deep seated and similar to the Western saddle. It is a good trail riding, all-purpose saddle and is used with a saddle pad underneath. It will fit almost any horse with a thick enough saddle pad underneath it.

If you ride Western saddle, your saddle will be heavy looking, although it is made to spread weight evenly. It has a deeper seat than any we have described, with high cantle and pommel. A horn to aid in roping cattle is at the head of the pommel. The leather is generally tooled and ornate and may have silver trappings. It may also have wide leather fenders that cover the stirrup leathers, and ornate leather coverings over the stirrups called tapaderos. Western saddles are also ridden with a Navajo blanket or a saddle pad underneath. These pads should fit well without wrinkling and be porous enough to absorb perspiration. You must keep them clean and well brushed.

Side saddles are still used by some women but rarely so in gaited events at horse shows. They are occasionally seen on hunters, jumpers and hunt teams. It is a very pleasant sight to see a woman mounted side saddle, but the way younger women are learning to ride astride, we doubt whether the side saddle will ever return to the popularity it once had.

There are many kinds of girths that you can use to hold the saddle in place. The girth is a band that passes under the belly of your horse and is fastened to "billets" on each side, underneath the skirt or flaps of your saddle.

Girths are generally made of web or leather, but sometimes are linen and angora hair. The web girth, clean and white, is proper for show or park purposes. There is a white tubular linen show girth made in England which is rubber lined and does not slip. The "Fitzwilliam" web girth is the double type, having three buckles. It is commonly used by show and breeding stables. For training needs, for hacking over country trails or foxhunting, the triple-folding leather girth with two buckles is most practical. It is strong and durable.

The Western saddle is generally equipped with girths known as "cinchas." They are usually made of strands of cotton, soft hair or mohair, with metal rings on each end. These are fastened to the cinch straps which are in turn attached to each side of the saddle.

With the exception generally of the Western saddle, you may purchase your saddle with or without stirrup leathers or irons. Stirrup irons should be large enough so that your shoe or boot will not be caught in case of spill, but still small enough to prevent your whole foot from slipping through. You can get irons especially adapted to the forward seat saddle. There are small rubber pads that fit into the botton of the stirrup irons that can be purchased for around $1.00 and will help to secure your foot. Safety stirrup irons may be used on children's saddles in which the iron unfastens and frees the foot in case of a spill.

Western saddles may have long and wide stirrup leathers that match the ornate design of the saddle, and wide wooden stirrups to accommodate the high-heeled boot so often worn. Just to keep the record straight, the cowboy was not the first to wear the high-heeled boot. And contrary to popular impression, he did not adopt it to prevent his foot from slipping through the stirrup. He took it over because the heel was handy to dig in the ground when roping cattle.

Actually, the soldiers of Genghis Khan, nearly 1000 years ago, wore high-heeled boots to make them appear taller and more fierce before their enemies. The cowboy boot is a colorful Western tradition and if you ride Western saddle, you may want to try the Western boot.

Now to clear up some fallacies regarding another piece of Western equipment—the spur. This chunk of iron, jutting out from your heel, is an instrument of torture when worn by an inexperienced rider. Even if worn only for looks, it is difficult to keep from jabbing your horse accidentally. Imagine yourself being stabbed in the loin with such a weapon even if the points are filed down.

Competent instructors will not permit their students to wear

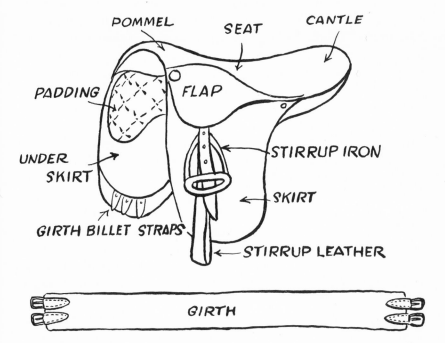

POMMEL   SEAT   CANTLE

PADDING   FLAP

UNDER SKIRT

STIRRUP IRON

SKIRT

GIRTH BILLET STRAPS

STIRRUP LEATHER

GIRTH

FIG. 21   The illustration above indicates parts of a flat saddle and girth.

spurs until they are adept in all phases of horsemanship. At this time a spur with a quarter-inch shank, but without a rowl, might be used with a sluggish mount. The need might occur in jumping, playing polo or encouraging the Walking Horse to maintain a steady running walk. Properly used, the spur is a reminder, not punishment. Cavalry men wore spurs for dress but seldom for actual use. We have found that a touch of the heel is nearly always as effective as a jab with a spur.

Before shopping for your bridle, you first should know exactly what you want, unless of course you are experimenting with bits in order to find the one most suitable for your horse. The reins, bits and headstall compose the bridle. The different types of bridles commonly used are the Weymouth or double bridle, snaffle, Pelham, Walking Horse and Western. The one you choose depends on how you are using your horse, his training and how tender or sensitive his mouth may be.

The bridle most commonly used on the Saddle Bred and others for bridle path and show is the double bridle. It is not too severe when properly used and is composed of the snaffle or bradoon and the curb bits. The snaffle and bradoon are similar, the snaffle being two short bars joined with a small ring in the center, and the bradoon having only one straight bar. On each end of the bit are large rings where the reins are attached. These bits have little or no severity. The horse has freedom to carry his head high or low.

The curb bit is a solid bar with a small curve in the center called a port. This bit rests on the tender bars of the mouth and has a curb chain exerting pressure under the chin. The cheek pieces of the curb bit have a ring at both ends. The ring at the upper end is attached to the headstall and the ring at the lower end is attached to the rein. When you pull the rein, it is like pulling a lever exerting pressure on the mouth with the bit, and under the chin from the curb chain. It can be very severe if the reins are pulled tight. But with skilled hands using the reins lightly, and your horse trained to respond, it is ideal for keeping his head in position and for restraint. When using the two bits in the mouth together, the snaffle is to give your horse freedom in moving along with minimum restraint and the curb to keep him collected with his head up, and have maximum restraint. A leather guard may be purchased to cover the curb chain that fits under the chin.

In using the Weymouth type, or any other type of bridle for show, studs are used in place of buckles when practical. No piece of the bridle should be wider than one-half inch, yet must be strong and in good condition, so there will be no danger of any part giving way.

A few years ago, colored nosebands and browbands on bridles were used only by racing stables. Recently, however, owners of Saddle Horses have taken up the custom of showing their stable colors through this means.

The next type of bridle is the snaffle or hunting bridle. It is a single bit bridle commonly used for hunting, jumping or trail riding. For this bridle there are many types of snaffle or bradoon bits, which your dealer will be glad to show you. They range from the large three inch in diameter ringed snaffle bit, that is quite weighty and jointed, to the smaller type that is used with the curb bit in the Weymouth bridle.

The snaffle bits are straight, sliding, jointed, twisted, rubber or wood mouthed. The best way to familiarize yourself with these bits is to study them from a sales catalogue or over the counter at your dealer's. Each of the bits mentioned has a different use, but you can seldom, if ever, hurt your horse's mouth if you use a large snaffle bit. However, many horses would be quite difficult to control without some degree of severity. Hence the double bridle or the Pelham bridle, which we shall discuss later, may be used in riding hunters and jumpers.

The hunting snaffle bridle, reins and cheek pieces are sewn into rings of the bit for safety. There is only one set of reins and they are plaited to prevent them from slipping through the fingers. Horses are usually broken and gaited with the snaffle bit as it will not hurt the tender mouth of a colt. In this case it is not necessary to have large reins or sewn-in bits.

The "Pelham" bridle is used more for polo than anything else, though it may be used for hunting or park and country riding. It has a single bit with double reins and the bit can best be described as a combination of two bits, the snaffle and the curb. In other words, with the double bridle, the horse has a snaffle and a curb

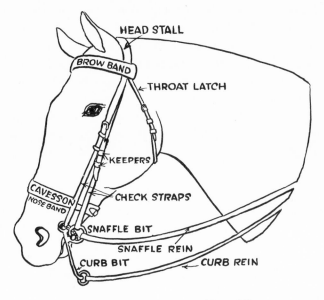

FIG. 22A   Parts of a Double Bridle.

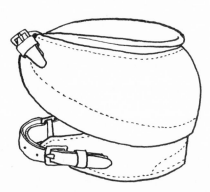

FIG. 22B   The Hinged Bell Quarter Boots are used extensively on the Five-Gaited Saddle Bred. They can be purchased at any riding equipment store for around eighteen dollars.

bit in his mouth, but with the Pelham he has only one bit. Its action, however, is like the two combined. One set of reins fits on loops joined to the curb bar itself and is severe. Pressure on this rein will make your horse respond instantly. The lower rein attachment to the end of the cheek piece gives the same freedom as the snaffle.

The Walking Horse bridle has one set of reins with a Walking Horse curb bit. It is similar to the bridle used for the Western type horse. The bit may have a slightly curved bar (low port) which fits between six to nine inch cheek pieces. These cheeks are often curved, and the rein fits on the lower end of the cheeks giving leverage. The longer shank, or cheek piece, helps to raise the head and keep the gaits true.

The Western bits are similar with long cheek pieces that may be silver, engraved or ornate. They are generally wider and curved in different shapes. They may have curb straps. One set of reins is used.

If you drive your horse or pony in fine harness, your leather bridle cheek should not be more than three-eighths of an inch wide and your lines only one inch wide. All harness equipment should be narrow, but strong and good grade leather.

Another piece of saddlery equipment that you may use is the martingale. The running-type martingale is most commonly used in training Saddle Breds. It will help to keep your horse's head down when he has a tendency to point out with his nose. The martingale is a strap attached under the belly, usually to the cincha by a hook in the end of the strap and running up between the horse's forelegs where it divides. These two straps extend up towards the neck of the horse on each side. The straps have rings on each end through which the reins or driving lines run.

Martingales are often used in training a horse to carry his head correctly, but are not used in gaited classes in the show ring. They may be used, if permitted, in jumping events. On your hunter, or jumper, either running or standing martingales may be used. The standing martingale is different in that the strap that runs between the forelegs continues as a single strap rather than dividing. It runs up under the chin where it is attached to the cavesson, which fits around his nose. This prevents your horse from throwing or tossing his head and gives you more control. Western martingales, called tie-downs, are similar to the standing martingale. They are usually prohibited in shows.

To secure your saddle in jumping, you may want to use a hunt-breastplate as it keeps the saddle from slipping backwards. It has a running martingale attachment with additional straps that run across the shoulders and back and fasten to the saddle.

Two other items of equipment you may need are a halter and a lead strap.

Quarter boots worn on the forefeet are standard equipment for the five-gaited Saddle Bred and should be worn at all times when riding or driving. The hinged quarter boot is most commonly used. This is important for many a gaited horse has suffered an injury or a "cut quarter" when the quarter boots were not used. The boot is of light weight leather and fits snugly around the hoof to prevent its being cut by the striding foot.

Young horses of any breed should wear quarter boots in early stages of training. The rubber glove type is satisfactory for this purpose.

If you drive your horse or pony, you will need a buggy. These are expensive, but fine harness classes are the highlight of a show.

A fine harness buggy is light, with only a seat and no top hood. It has chromium plated wheels and ball bearing spindles that make it travel easily and noiselessly. For the same price you can generally purchase a combination buggy for roadster, fine harness and combination classes. This buggy is not quite so light in appearance. The seat has a back and there is a top hood that can be let down. In this position, it extends back of the seat.

For driving your Shetland pony, you may use the viceroy buggy. Naturally it is smaller than the other two. It is of Victorian design and may be equipped with patent leather fenders and dash. Any miniature side rail buggy, however, similar to the fine harness, is appropriate.

You may also find you need a hunting crop and thong if you hunt the fox, and a buggy whip if you drive. The hunting crop, with a crooked handle, has a silk lash more than a yard long, called a thong. The crook of the handle is useful in opening gates

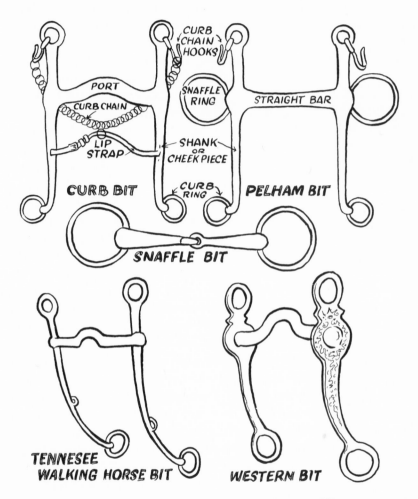

Fig. 23 Types of Bits Used with Different Bridles.

when in the hunting field, and the silken lash may be first aid equipment if needed.

Care of Saddlery

Care of saddlery, harness and other tack is an integral part of stable management. Many pages could be written about it, but rather than try to cover every phase, we will cover the important points which might seem confusing.

As far as tack is concerned, we have seen saddles and bridles that have been in almost constant use for more than thirty years. Despite the long use, they were in fine condition. This was due to proper care. Good leather, if given just a little better than ordinary care, will last the average non-professional pleasure rider a lifetime. Yet there are some people owning expensive horse equipment, who literally have to struggle to make it survive two seasons.

We will not go so far as to recommend the use of melted unsalted butter or vaseline to preserve the original color of the leather, but we urge you to follow definite routines with the equipment after it has been used.

Immediately after you use the leather tack, we suggest that you wipe it clean with a damp sponge. This will clean off dirt and grime and keep it looking better.

Frequently, you should wash your leather thoroughly with a good saddle soap. How often you do this depends on the frequency of use. Domestic saddle soaps are every bit as good as the imported and far more reasonable. To clean your tack properly, all the buckles and studs should be unfastened, for that is where the leather is subject to the severest wear. The directions on how to apply saddle soap are on the package. They usually instruct you to allow about fifteen minutes, after washing, to dry before rubbing with a dry cloth. If this method of soaping is followed, your leather goods should stay in excellent condition.

If you desire a bright finish on the leather, after washing apply a harness dressing. There are several good ones on the market that do not take long to apply. First, go over the leather with a damp cloth to remove the dirt if you have not just finished soaping.

Then, dip a small sponge in the dressing and go over the leather. The dressing will dry quickly and leave a high lustre.

In order to keep your leather pliable and workable, it must contain a certain amount of oil. It should first be oiled when it is new. There are several opinions on how a new piece of saddlery should be treated. Some persons, especially the Englishmen we have talked with, use oil very sparingly and rely solely upon the oil and glycerine in saddle soap. Others will take a new bridle and immerse it in a pan of oil before using. Still others will go over all the new leather with a sponge soaked in Neat's Foot Oil. We agree with the latter and suggest that it be used in the following manner. Wipe the new piece of tack with a clean cloth and go over it with a small sponge that has been moistened in Neat's Foot Oil. Oiling of straps and skirts may be done on the rough under surface rather than on the smooth, outer finish. The leather will absorb the oil and your clothing is better protected. Repeat this in about a week and again two weeks later. The frequency with which you oil your equipment will depend on the use it receives. You should oil it often enough to keep it pliable and prevent cracking. The Englishman's greatest argument against oil is that the oiled seat and skirt of his saddle will soil his light hunting breeches.

Nothing aids more in making a horse look well groomed than correctly cleaned and cared for harness. It also is a reflection upon you as an owner.

If a strap should break or a seam rip loose, take that piece of equipment to the harness maker at once to be repaired. Do not be careless about such things, for if a piece of damaged equipment is not repaired immediately, it might become damaged beyond repair, or be the cause of a bad accident. Either would be expensive. You must be especially careful of this if you jump your horse.

Bridles and harness are best preserved when not in use by hanging and covering with a sheet to protect them from dust, dirt and ammonia fumes from the stable. Saddles should be hung on brackets. They are made by stable equipment manufacturers, and are reasonably priced. They permit the air to get to the underside of the saddle. This prevents mold from forming or the leather from cracking, and thereby lengthens the life of the saddle. The tree of your saddle is its backbone. Care must be taken that it does not become bent or broken.

Bits and stirrup irons should also be washed and wiped clean before they are allowed to dry. Metal polish or dampened sand can be used to restore their brilliance. The shafts and wheels of your cart or buggy should also be washed or cleaned immediately after use and the wheels kept greased.

Strive at all times to have your leather in good condition. A well turned out horse is a sight to see, so do not detract from your mount by not keeping your equipment in top shape. This is just as important on the bridle paths as it is at shows.

CHAPTER VIII

Breeding

In this chapter we will endeavor to prove that you don't need to be wealthy to have a breeding establishment of your own. You don't even need to own a stallion. One or more mares and a place to keep them is all that is actually needed, plus some "know how" on your part.

We do want to caution you, however, that breeding horses of show calibre is a business for professionals and you as an amateur are a long way from a professional or a scientific breeder. Before attempting to breed, you should have had considerable experience handling horses, and it would then be wise to have access to the advice of a more experienced horseman or breeder.

There is room for more amateur breeders all over the country, both for pleasure and profit, if you have had the proper experience. Even though you may not produce a top show horse, you can be pretty sure of getting a fine pleasure mount. Even the experienced breeders of the Thoroughbred for racing, who carefully study bloodlines of sires and dams who have supplied winners, are said by the Racing Association to average only about 37% of the horses produced ever reaching the race track. So don't expect to get a perfect colt.

You may ask, "Why breed your mare when you can buy a good colt or filly for so much less than it would cost to raise one?" We can only state that there is a certain pride of ownership in raising your own colt. There is a feeling in watching him grow that can only be experienced by those who have actually raised and trained a colt of their own. It is commonly said among horsemen that you have never really owned a horse until you have bred, raised and trained one.

It is not necessary, except in cases of breeding farms or on large estates, to own a stallion for breeding purposes. In the first place, a stallion does not often make a good riding horse, especially

116

when around other horses. In hunter classes at shows, riding stallions is forbidden. An amateur would not want the extra expense of keeping a stallion. Then too, if one purchases the services of a stallion, he can pick out the one he thinks would make the most suitable cross for his mare or mares. This is particularly important if you want to improve certain points of conformation in the progeny of your mare, or wish to breed to a stallion that has produced a long line of jumpers, or if breeding for color in case of the Palomino.

Even the largest of the breeding stables do not always use their own stallions. Some of the brood mares are invariably sent out to other stallions to bring new blood into the stable. This service is sometimes exchanged but usually has to be paid for.

If you are troubled with the problem of getting a stallion, the Secretary of the Breeders' Association of the horse you have, will be glad to advise you regarding location of stallions. The various horse magazines also carry advertisements from breeders all over the country.

When not gratis, the fee for service will generally run from ten dollars to five hundred, depending on the stallion. Among Thoroughbreds it may run more. The size of the fee depends on the foals the stallion has sired in the past. Lengthy studies have been made of bloodlines of the different breeds and some lines seem to cross better than others to produce fine animals. This is why breeding is difficult. As an amateur, you may be after only a good pleasure horse and not concerned with fine show horses. However, it is a good idea to study the different bloodlines and crosses if you are planning to breed. You may need the help of an experienced breeder as bloodlines are worked out in charts. Among Saddle Breds, for example, over the years the lines have become so crossed and mixed that it is difficult to trace them. Some breeders of this breed feel they are becoming too closely interbred or related and believe an infusion of Standardbred blood at this time would improve the trot and other gaits.

Among the Saddle Bred Stallions for the year 1939, the service fee for *Kalarama Rex,* who had the highest rating for sires, in the stallion poll taken by a Saddle Horse Magazine, was $150.00 to approved mares for that year. The rating was figured from points his sons and daughters earned at the various large shows that year. Today it would probably cost you more to breed to this calibre stallion.

For your mare to be approved, she would have to meet certain standards set by the stallion's owner. Generally, she must be of a bloodline known to cross well with that of the stallion and free of defects and bad faults of conformation that she might pass to a foal.

If you are in search of a good pleasure mount rather than a high class show horse, you may obtain services of less well known stallions for a much smaller fee. It must be understood, however, that unless you are an experimental breeder seeking to improve the breed, or in search of an ideal weight carrying hunter, or breeding small horses to ponies or vice versa for pony size, you should breed your mare to a stallion of the same breed. This means a Saddle Bred mare to a Saddle Bred stallion, Tennessee Walking Horse to Tennessee Walking Horse, Arab to Arab. Generally, as with humans, larger horses will beget larger horses. However, it will not run true in every instance. If you are breeding for a hunter, you will naturally consider the weight carrier you want him to be. You would not want a horse too light for you. If you are looking for a heavy weight, you may succeed with a mare of large bone and a stallion equally as large or larger. Some breeders will use the Percheron in attempting to get a heavy weight Half-Bred.

In any event, if breeding for a Half-Bred hunter or jumper, you will want to breed for stamina and substance. To register your Half-Bred in the Half-Bred Registry, the stallion you use must be Thoroughbred. If you are breeding for a three-gaited horse, you will try to get a feminine, peacocky type of good quality. But if for a five-gaited horse, a more bold, fiery, handsome type is desirable.

The breeds breeders use in producing Half-Bred hunters and jumpers may vary somewhat by locality and according to the prevalence of breeds in the area. In the West, breeders often breed Quarter Horses and range horses to Thoroughbreds, whereas in the East, Hackneys or coach horses, Cleveland Bays, Morgans, Saddle Breds and others are more widely used.

There are breeders who argue the merits of the Half-Bred

and Thoroughbred as working hunters. They argue that the Thoroughbred has such great heart he will never give up on a hunt, whereas others say the Half-Bred will go equally as far. We might suggest that every horse is different and no matter what cross you may want, or what you want in breeding to the same breed, you should consider the bloodline and conformation of the stallion you choose. Attempt to breed for good qualities that your mare might not possess. This can best be done when you are able to select your own stallion.

Col. John F. Wall, of the U. S. Army Remount Service, who has studied breeding exhaustively, says that "almost without exception conformation, performance and bloodlines go hand in hand." Consequently, it is good to keep this in mind when breeding your mare.

The mare you intend to breed should be checked for soundness before breeding. By that we mean sound in the qualities she will most likely pass along to the foal. Drawing from Mr. Clarence Bosworth's experience in breeding, the probable "get" from a Saddle Bred and Thoroughbred cross would be a Saddle Bred type with more quality but less action and brilliance than a pure Saddle Bred. This foal would doubtless make a fair hunter, jumper, hunter hack and possibly a polo prospect. If you use a Thoroughbred mare and a Saddle Bred stallion the "get" would likely be Saddle Bred type, with more brilliance and action, with improved substance and stamina than if crossed in the reverse way. Thoroughbreds have founded several breeds. Like the Arab, they are used to improve quality.

A Saddle Bred mare and Arab stallion would probably get reduced size and bad type, although it might produce a flashy mount for young riders, a bridle path hack or a fair jumper. Welsh stallions crossed with Arab mares get excellent children's hunters, jumpers and hacks.

If you are breeding for a pony, you must be careful that your foal will not grow beyond 14.2 hands and go out of the pony class. Some experts believe they get better results in breeding ponies and small horses for pony size, by breeding the stallion to a pony mare. However, we have also seen good results from the reverse cross. For ponies, it is best not to breed both stallion and mare who are around 14 hands as there is too much risk of their foal developing beyond the 14.2 limit.

It is often said there are no perfect horses. This may be so, but with your mare you are after the best you can get. Do not hesitate to ask the advice of a reliable horseman. He will be glad to help and advise you regarding the location and "get" of a stallion the same breed as your mare. After looking at your mare, he will help you in trying to secure the services of a stallion that might be able to improve some faults in comformation.

In breeding to a stallion, you should not only know what the service fee will be but have some contract or guarantee regarding the living foal. In Thoroughbreds the service fee sometimes runs into large sums and often no guarantee whatsoever is given. The contract or guarantee regarding a living foal varies with different stallion owners. Before having your mare serviced, you should have a satisfactory agreement—in writing—with the owner. This should include a provision for your mare's board should she stay any length of time at the stable of the stallion.

There are different kinds of guarantees that owners of stallions make with mare owners. Some agree to produce a living foal, some just the foal, while others agree to produce a foal to stand and suck. It is always best to know before breeding just what the guarantee and fee will be for the stallion chosen. The fee and board bill generally is paid before the mare leaves the farm or place where she was bred. The stallion owner usually relieves himself from any liability regarding accidents or escapes. Should your mare need any veterinary care, you are responsible for the charges.

After your mare has been serviced, be sure to get a Breeder's Certificate from the owner of the stallion in order that the foal may be registered with the Secretary of its respective breed, if it is eligible.

We have heard many horsemen state when asked if his horse was registered: "He can write his own registration; he can really turn on and run in the money anywhere." This may be true, but again we say, you as an amateur are a long way from a professional breeder. Nine times out of ten, if the horse mentioned were eligible for registration, he would have been registered. The only exception might be in the case of a gelding, for the gelding cannot reproduce.

Registering does give a genuine feeling of ownership and we recommend that you immediately register your foals if they are eligible. The registration fee is nominal and if at some later date it becomes necessary to sell the foal, it would be a shame to spoil the sale or have to take a lower price because the prospective purchaser wanted a horse "with papers."

For recording purposes, all registered horses are one year old on January first following the date of foaling. It is better that the foal be born in the spring so he can run with the dam during the summer months in order that he might graze and gain strength. The period of gestation in mares is 340 days. There are many contrary superstitions, founded mainly because an accurate date of the service was not kept. Do not fail to mark down the date of service. The foal may be dropped a few days early or late.

If your mare is healthy before breeding, do not change her feed or give her balls or laxatives just because you are going to breed her. If she has been wintering on hay alone, she should be started on a grain ration prior to being bred. If your mare has never before been bred, do not let anyone prepare her by inserting their arm or hand before "cover." This is absolutely unnecessary and might prove harmful. The owners of the stallion will know how to take care of your mare as they have had lots of experience in this field.

After the mare has been serviced, it is best to walk her until she regains her composure. This will only take a few minutes. Do not let her stop and strain for she might expel the spermatozoa. When she has quieted down, she should be washed externally around the genital parts with cold water containing some mild antiseptic.

After she is bred, keep using your mare at whatever she has been doing up to this time, not roughly but with consideration. Also continue to ride and exercise her. During the last two months before foaling, dispense with all strenuous exercise.

There is no way of telling whether you will get a colt or a filly. Science says this is only determined by the ovum of the mare.

The time of service or "where the moon was at the time" makes no difference in this matter. There has always been much discussion as to whether the sire or the dam was predominant in characteristics passed to the foal. The most qualified horsemen agree that both the sire and dam contribute equally in passing on their qualities to the foal. However, you may note many Thoroughbred followers who say the sire predominates and others who say the dam contributes sixty percent.

Your mare should not be "force bred," except on advice of a veterinarian. She should be bred during her heat period when she will stand quietly for the stallion. The way to tell when she is in heat is to have her in contact with the stallion or "teaser" every day, then service her on the first day she will submit. Mares are in heat at different times, although usually about every twenty-one days. It might be a longer interval or as often as every fourteen days. Your mare should be returned to the stallion seven days after she has first submitted. If she will not stand at this time, try her again five days later. If she refuses after the second try, you may be reasonably sure that she is in foal. If convenient, another attempt should be made seven days after the second try.

Gole and Hart in 1930 pioneered the injection of blood from pregnant mares into immature animals for testing pregnancy in mares. They found these injections caused changes in the reproductive organs of these animals. Tests were also made with urine. Colonel John F. Wall and Dr. Edward Horgan have gone on with these experiments and have found that the test cannot be made until forty days after the mare has been bred. They hope to find a test that will give a positive reaction of pregnancy at an earlier date.

Thirty days before your mare is due to foal, she should be relieved of all duty, and if possible, turned out to pasture during the day. At this time, if your mare does not already have one, she should have a roomy box stall that is clean and airy and has a good, soft bed. Cleanliness in the barn is an important requisite if the mare is going to foal there. The stall should be completely cleaned out and disinfected about three days before the foal is due.

You should now begin to watch your mare closely about fifteen days before she is due to foal. When a discharge appears, wash her parts daily with warm water. It is best at this time to feed carrots and bran mash, especially for the three or four days immediately prior to foaling. Do not leave a halter or stable sheet on her at this time.

When labor begins, your mare will become very restless, going round and round her stall and continually will be getting up and down. The labor period is very short. The mare will sweat and lie down and then finally expel the foal, front feet and head first. If the cord does not break, cut it about six inches from the foal's body and paint it with iodine immediately.

Now wipe the mare and foal dry with straw or towels. If the foal does not appear to be doing well, a little artificial respiration might stimulate its circulation. The mare will be up on her feet by this time, so after cleaning out the soiled bedding, wash the mare's genital parts with warm water and leave the two to get acquainted.

Of course the procedure just discussed was for a normal birth. If the mare has been trying unsuccessfully for more than an hour to expel the foal and it does not appear, summon your veterinarian.

Should the foal not start to suck in about fifteen minutes, lift his head toward the teats and usually this will be all that is necessary.

If the bowels of the foal do not move within twelve hours after birth, insert your finger and a little mineral oil in the rectum. If they do not move within a few hours after this treatment or if there is a watery discharge, call your veterinarian. If the mare's milk does not agree with the foal, your veterinarian can prescribe a substitute which will most likely be cow's milk and lime water.

After a month has passed, give the foal his own feed box and have it set a bit lower than the dam's. With this arrangement they will not interfere with each other while eating.

We suggest foaling in the barn. In the event that something unforeseen happens and the mare needs assistance she can be cared for. Many breeders will take issue with us on this and say that for hundreds of years mares have been bringing their young into the world out in the open with Mother Nature for a nurse. This is true, but we have heard of cases where foals were lost because of accidents when the mares were allowed to foal in pasture. Dr. H. J. Meyer of Saginaw, Michigan, told us about a foaling in which the filly would have suffocated, had he not been there to break the sac when it was born.

There should be very little handling of the new foal, just enough to accustom him to you and keep him from developing fear of human beings. At the Fox Hollow Farm in Orange, Virginia, a halter is put on young Welsh foals for a few minutes, almost before they are actually dry. Ponies are handled lightly from the very beginning and become used to the human as well as the halter. They find with this method they never have to break them.

Many good trainers prefer to slip a small halter on the colt at least two to three days after he is foaled. At this age there is never a struggle. In doing this, be careful not to leave the halter on too long. The young foal might get himself entangled. In addition, his skin is very tender and will easily bruise. After he becomes accustomed to the halter, you may begin teaching him to lead.

Have someone lead the mare while you take the colt's halter and follow behind. You may halt the colt from time to time and have your helper lead the mare on. When the mare is a few paces away, urge the colt forward with the halter and catch up with the mare. After a few days of this, you may even lead the colt in a different direction from the mare and he will not put up a struggle.

Be very careful at this early stage not to frighten him as your object is to instill confidence. You must be patient and gentle with him, speaking with a smooth, kindly voice, but always exercise firmness. Demand that your colt obey you from the very beginning and never let him get away with doing as he pleases.

During his first year he needs time to grow and to run with his dam in pasture. About all you should attempt to teach him in this period is to be caught, to allow his halter to be placed on him, to lead, and to stand for grooming and care of his feet.

Teaching him to be caught in pasture is generally accomplished by haltering the mare and bringing them both to a corner. Maneuver so that the mare will be on the outside and the foal in the corner. You will need a helper at first, but with the foal already accustomed to being haltered and led around the barn area, you

FIG. 24   The Shetland foal becomes the pet of even a four-year-old. They are gentled from birth when handled young. Notice how easily the young foal can be caught in pasture when offered grain.

FIG. 25 Handle the young colt early. Teach him to lead and stand quietly. Thus he learns not to fear you and is more amenable to your will.

will not have much trouble. Also offering a little grain in the feed bucket will help in the beginning.

After you have trained him to lead quietly and stand still when you are holding his halter or lead strap, you can begin teaching him to stand in cross-ties. You should have a helper with this. Lead him to the passageway of the barn and have your helper hand you the cross-tie ropes. Fasten them easily to his halter. Work very calmly and quietly. Have your assistant then stand behind him and you stand in front. If he starts to move forward, stop him. If he starts to move backward, your assistant should stop him. In this way he learns to stand in cross-ties to be brushed lightly and have his feet picked up.

In the beginning it is best to run your hand down easily from the top of his leg almost to his foot and pick it up. Start with his near foreleg. Brace your body against his hindquarter when picking up his hind foot and he will be less apt to kick. After he will let you handle his feet, you can keep them picked out and rasped level. Starting these things early will make your colt much easier to handle.

Most breeders suggest feeding him a little grain even while he is running with his mother. You might begin with a handful and gradually work up to a quart twice a day. Most colts are weaned at six months.

Professional trainers frown on keeping colts too much in the barnyard, and feeding them sugar and tidbits. They maintain that colts raised in this close environment more readily develop vices, become stubborn and inclined to nudge and nip when you appear without the tidbit.

Some trainers prefer not to bother with the colt after his early handling until he is a yearling or even two years old. The horse does not forget his early associations. Since you are an amateur, we believe it better that you handle your colt frequently. He will be much easier for you to manage.

The foal will give you lots of excitement and worry during his first year—but that is only the beginning. He is yours. You have bred him and now you are raising him. There will be the training, the gaiting, jumping or whatever else you plan for your horse to do, and many years of pleasure ahead for both of you.

CHAPTER IX

Training

From the beginning let us caution you as we did with breeding that unless you have had considerable experience handling horses, or will have the help of an experienced trainer, you will find it difficult to train your own colt. You cannot teach what you do not know yourself.

However, if your love of horses runs deep enough, and you have the experience and patience, you can do the job. We have seen amateurs produce some fine show horses and pleasure mounts because of their hard work. If you can possibly handle the task, we strongly advocate it for you are sure to have a closer bond with any horse you handle, care for and school.

If you are a newcomer to the horse fraternity, endeavoring to learn, we hope that training as we discuss it here will give you a greater appreciation of the effort that goes into making your mount a well mannered performer.

It is well to say at the start that we will offer no advice on how to make your horse kneel, roll over, kick you or "bark like a dog." Tricks are not hard to teach but we suggest you spend your time wisely on schooling your mount in manners and gaits.

Should you ask several professional trainers of any breed how they go about training their horse, all of them would doubtless give you a slightly different method. Yet each of them might produce winners in the show ring. One horseman will rigidly practice techniques that another will completely discredit. Therefore when we discuss training, the methods we suggest are either what we have found in our own experience to be useful, or have known other experienced horsemen to use effectively. We do not offer these as the only way, for many are certain to disagree with us. As one splendid horseman once remarked: "There is more than one way to skin a cat and the same is true in training horses. There is no absolute method."

FIG. 26 A "bitting rig." (The reins shown forward from the mouth are merely for purposes of this photography.) Notice the two straps attached to the snaffle bit, one running up the cheek piece and attached to the upper part of the harness. The lower straps are attached further down on the bellyband. The lower strap illustrated here is very loose. This is a new experience for the young colt. When he accepts the "rig," begin to tighten the straps. The lower strap will be taut and much shorter than is illustrated here. Thus the colt cannot extend his chin because of the strap. As he learns, both straps are gradually shortened, the upper one raises his head and the lower one brings his chin in.

In the first place, every horse is different and takes special handling, just as humans have individual characteristics and temperaments. Differences in the conformation of both horse and trainer also influence methods of training and handling. Horses being trained for show are more carefully finished than pleasure horses, regardless of breed. Their finished training becomes as technical as teaching an athlete to box.

The way you train your horse will depend largely on how you plan to use him, whether for show, hunting, park riding or on the trail. We train the horse to do the job we want. He is quick to learn, as he learns by association and habit. He is willing to do what you ask when you let him know what you want, and by constant repetition begins to perfect his performance. His sensitiveness to touch creates a medium through which you can teach him to respond with certain movements. When touched on different parts of his body, or feeling the bit in his mouth, he learns to associate what he feels with his actions. As we shall see later in teaching the Saddle Bred his gaits, he will associate the direction he is going with a specific gait.

You must be firm in your training process and demand that your horse obey you, or you will never be successful as a trainer. Any experienced horseman will warn you never to let a horse get away with doing as he pleases. Always demand that he do any task asked. Make him repeat it until he does and then reward him with a pat on the neck.

In early training you must be especially careful not to frighten your pupil. Proceed slowly and cautiously with anything new. Use kindness and patience. Remember the horse doesn't understand the words you say but he does understand the tone in which you say them.

In this chapter we will discuss training as it varies with the different breeds and types of horses being used for different purposes. First, we will consider training of the Saddle Bred as an example for saddle horse type. And we want to emphasize that you can apply the basic principles of this training in the walk, trot and canter to any saddle horse ridden in three-gaited events or driven in fine harness where action is desire. It matters not whether he is Morgan or Arab. In three-gaited events under Eng-

lish saddle it is equally important for the Morgan and Arab
to exhibit high natural action and collection.

Second, we will take up the Tennessee Walking Horse, which
has his own unique way of going in the running walk; third, the
hunter, jumper and hunter hack will be studied. This generally
includes the Thoroughbred, whose natural ability to jump and
move across country at a low striding gallop is developed through
training. Fourth, we will study the Western type horse or any
horse trained to be ridden under Western saddle. This commonly
includes the Western horse of mixed origin and of different types
and colors, the Quarter Horse, Thoroughbred, Morgan, Arab and
Appaloosa. And finally, we will discuss training of the pony for
children.

SCHOOLING THE AMERICAN SADDLE BRED

Your Saddle Bred colt will be ready to start serious training
after he has reached two years of age and has learned to lead well
on the halter. We think the best first step is to break him to the
"bitting rig" while in his box stall.

The "bitting rig" is a combination of bridle, harness pad and
crupper. Its purpose is to teach the horse to flex at the poll, that
is to bend his neck near the top of his head so his chin is tucked.
Such flexions of the head and neck are important and a prime
requisite in a show horse.

The bridle of the "bitting rig" should have a large jointed or
plain snaffle bit. A strap buckling to the bit runs to the belly band
or harness pad. This strap can be taken up or lengthened. Also
buckled to the bit is another line called a side check which runs
up the side of the cheek piece of the bridle through a ring just
above the throat latch, across the top of the harness pad, where it
is caught by a steel loop to hold it in place. It runs similarly around
the other side of the bit. The side check can also be lengthened
and taken up at the buckles so as to place your horse's head where
you want it. Notice the "bitting rig" pictured in Figures 26 and
27.

The head should not be checked too high and the side straps
should be even and quite loose so that the colt can flex more at the
poll by himself. This will tend to keep him from fretting and

Fɪɢ. 27   This illustrates the "bitting rig" on a finished horse. He is being longed in the "rig" to practice flexation and correct head carriage. Notice how his neck is arched just behind the ears and his chin is tucked. His head position is much different from that of the beginning colt illustrated in Figure 26. The above "rig" is improvised from a Weymouth or double bridle with the snaffle rein doubled back up the cheek strap and run through a loop near the throat latch so that it can then be fastened to a terret on the harness pad. The curb rein runs from the bit to the bellyband or may be tied over the neck as shown here by Walt McCallie, trainer.

Courtesy Mrs. J. U. Elliot and Mrs. C. Z. Board
Photo by Ivan Mashek

Fig. 28 The two amateurs above demonstrate technique of schooling the young colt to move in a circle on a longe line for the first time. The trainer moves around with the horse on a short line until he begins to learn. The helper leads him from the halter on the opposite side.

fighting the rig. His head will be in a somewhat unnatural position, different from the way he has freely carried it up to now. As he gradually gets used to the rig, the side straps may be taken up a notch or two to further hold his head up. For the first few lessons, five to ten minutes is long enough to leave him in the harness as it will tire him. The time may be increased as the young horse learns and ceases objecting to it.

The "bitting rig" should not be used for the first time unless you are accompanied by a person who has had experience with it, so that you will not get the colt's head too high at first. You must slip the rig on carefully, talking to the young horse kindly and petting him so that he won't fear this strange new object. You will need help with the maneuver. The "rig" is a very useful piece of tack, but in the wrong hands can be dangerous to the future of a young horse.

We suggest using a web "bitting harness" as it is much cheaper than leather. It can be bought for $25.00.

From wearing the "bitting harness" your colt will become accustomed to the feel of the bit in his mouth, which has been a well chosen snaffle. When he reaches this stage, he is ready to be started on the longe line. He will continue wearing the "bitting rig" to which the longe line can be attached.

Your purpose in exercising him on the longe is to make him obedient to your commands and to go under your control. By schooling in the rig, he is also learning to go flexed at the poll. He learns to stop and go, to walk and trot, as well as to turn at your command. It accustoms him to going on a line in preparation for further training in long-lines and eventual hitching, where you will have even greater control.

A cotton web line, 1⅛ inches wide by 20 to 30 feet long, with a hand loop on one end and a swivel snap on the other, will serve your purpose and cost you less than five dollars. (See Figure 27.) The longe line can also be an ordinary rope, fastened under the chin to a rope halter as pictured in Figure 28. In this case the horse is longed without the "bitting rig."

If using the "rig," some trainers run the web longe line through the ring of the bit on the near side, up the cheek piece over the head and down the cheek piece on the off side, snapping it to the bit. By attaching it in this way the bit will remain steady in the colt's mouth and not be pulling to one side with pressure on the line.

To longe your colt take up the length of your line in several loops so that you will be only three or four feet away from the horse with the line taut. Hold the loops between the thumb and forefinger of the left hand, which frees your right hand for carrying a whip. You will need a whip. Stand opposite your horse's quarters and have someone hold him on the off side at the bit. As you command him to GET-UP have your helper lead him forward in a small circle. Walk along with him about his shoulder. (See Figure 28.) As he learns, feed out your loops and let him go in a larger circle. Your object is to have him go around you in a circle at the end of your 20 or 30 foot line. (See Figure 29.)

Stop him often to WHOA and start him again to GET-UP. Keep him at a walk. In this way he learns to answer your commands. Also teach him to turn. A Saddle Bred may turn either toward the rail or away from it when he reverses in the show ring, so you may turn either to the inside or outside of your circle. When you turn him in the opposite direction, attach the longe line to the opposite side of his bit.

When he is going around you, starting and stopping on your command, your helper can move away from his head. If he stops without being told, moving your whip in your right hand is generally enough to keep him going. When you are ready to increase his pace by commanding him to trot, at the same time shake your line slightly. He will come to associate TROT with his trotting movement.

After you have him answering your voice commands and can increase and decrease his pace, you will not need your helper. Exercising the colt in this way, you will notice how he becomes increasingly easy to control. He is also learning to carry his head correctly.

Trainers of the Saddle Bred do not spend so much time longeing as for some other breeds. They soon move on to preparation for hitching and driving by first breaking him to harness with long lines. He will now have a line attached to each side of his snaffle bit and will be driven with these lines. It is best that the harness

Courtesy Mrs. C. Z. Board
Photo by Ivan Mashek

FIG. 29   The colt learns to circle around the trainer on a 20 to 30 foot line answering to voice commands to walk, trot, canter, whoa and turn. This exercise helps him to be more supple and to gain better flexation of the head and neck whether or not the "bitting rig" is used.

first be put on in the barn and the colt then led out into the training area. He will doubtless be fidgety and want to play or get
loose. Have an assistant walk along at his head, leading him while
you get behind with the reins. At first you can walk a little to the
inside with the reins across his back but as he learns you can begin
to drive him from directly behind. You will have to be firm but
gentle. Soon the colt will go along by himself. (See Figures 30
and 31.)

Keep him at a walk, stopping at frequent intervals, then urging him on again. Begin turning him frequently in different directions and make some figure eights. You are now teaching him
to turn easily and be guided in answer to signals from your reins.
Heretofore he has learned to answer only your voice. Now if you
want him to turn left, you pull on the left rein. Do the opposite
for the right turn.

While walking behind the colt, it is well to remember to allow
the reins to fall on each side of the horse near the stifle bone.
In this way, if he has a tendency to turn his hindquarters, you will
have enough control to straighten him out with the reins. Your
object is to keep his body straight as he moves forward. If he rears
and you are on soft ground, pull him over on his back. This will
not be to his liking and one or two times on his back will cure
him of this vice.

After your colt has gained some confidence, you might start
him at a slow trot. Encourage him by talking to him. This will
be tiring for you running behind, but after a few days of this, he
should be ready to hitch. Before hitching, however, have him shod
with light plates of five or six ounces. This will give him balance
and action.

A two-wheeled breaking cart with long shafts is best for hitching. Oftentimes the colt will try to get away and a runaway at
this time must be avoided above all things. If he does get away,
you will have a hard time trying to convince him that he is not
to bolt as soon as he is hitched. Have a good strong harness and
be sure he is harnessed properly.

After you have hitched the colt, it is best to commence the
same as you did when you first harnessed him. Have someone walk
at the colt's head so you can walk behind with the reins. Also have

someone push the cart along at first. Should the colt feel a pull against his harness, he is apt to get the impression he is tied and bolt. Stop him and turn him often. As no two horses are alike, it will have to be left to your own judgment when to get into the cart and when to have the person leading let go. In any event, we suggest that you wait to get into the cart until the colt begins to accept being hitched to it and is settled down, moving calmly forward at a walk. Your colt will be easily frightened so you should proceed as quietly as possible.

The first few hitchings should be for short periods and just at a walk. As the young horse gains confidence, he can be put into a slow trot, then gradually extended. There is nothing like hitching and driving to develop your colt's speed in a sound square trot. The Saddle Bred uses his shoulders for his drive and action. Harness driving helps him to use and pull on his shoulders, developing them along with good balance.

Try not to be impatient as all of this takes time and depends largely on your colt's aptness to learn.

After he is well broken to the cart, and if close to three years old, you can get ready to saddle him. Lay a blanket or sack over him first to get him used to something being on his back. Also let him smell and nuzzle his saddle to get him acquainted with it. After he shows no signs of fear of these objects, remove the stirrup leathers and irons from the saddle and lay it on his back. Do not fasten the girth too tightly.

After your horse has become accustomed to the saddle, then you can prepare to mount. You may do as some trainers, tie a sack of feed on the saddle for short periods for the first two or three times. Then you can put the leathers and irons on the saddle and lean your body across it without mounting, resting your weight on the saddle. If your horse does not object to this, you may have an assistant hold his head and boost yourself into the saddle. When mounting for the first time, the colt will probably take this right in stride as so many new things have been happening to him.

If you have not previously broken horses, we suggest that for this first time at least, you get a more experienced horseman to mount for you. After all, you do not want to hurt the colt's mouth

Courtesy Mrs. J. U. Elliot and Mrs. C. Z. Board
Photo by Ivan Mashek

FIG. 30   In the above picture, the helper is leading the colt in his beginning lesson in long lines. The trainer walks slightly to the inside about even with the hindquarters. Notice how the colt is obstructed from attention to the trainer if the helper leads on the inside. Thus the helper should always lead from the offside.

FIG. 31 As the colt learns, the trainer drives him from directly behind. Saddle Bred trainers spend much time driving in long lines in preparation for hitching to a cart.

by pulling on it at this early date, and this could very easily happen.

Five minutes or so at a walk is enough for the first time. Mount him again the next day and gradually increase the exercise periods. He will be quite excited and lather up but pet him often and speak encouragingly to him. Try not to put any more pressure on the rein while mounted or driving than he has been used to with the "bitting rig." In a few days he will trot out by himself and you can let him have his own way a little for the first few times under saddle.

When your colt has become accustomed to having you on his back, which should take at least a week or more, and you have let him do just about as he pleases, you are ready to start training him in his gaits.

After saddling, do not discontinue the driving. Keep driving him at least twice a week, if possible. You will never regret this driving later and his gaits will show it. Five times a week is often enough to work your young horse. He needs a lot of energy to grow and fill out. Do not work it all out of him. If you are driving twice a week, three times will be often enough to ride him. This will give him two days to rest, but try not to have these rest days come together.

Now comes the most important part. Unless your horse in conformation is unmistakably a walk-trot or three-gaited type, we presume you will want to teach him the five gaits of the American Saddle Bred. They are walk, trot, canter, slow gait and rack. Each of these gaits is as important as the other, including the walk which too often is passed over lightly. Your horse will not be five-gaited if he is unable to do any of these mentioned gaits later on.

To begin schooling him in his gaits, you may start while walking him to and from his place of training. It is a good time to work on his walk and the holding up and flexing of his head at the poll. Endeavor at all times to keep him collected, that is alert, "on his toes," with his mind on his business, ready to respond. Do not let his walk become sloppy.

At the walk, we again emphasize that his feet must be picked up with energy and carried over in a straight line from one point of contact to the next. Both his knees and ankles must flex or bend and his hocks are carried well under his body. His walk must be lively and vigorous.

From noting the training methods of several well known trainers of the Saddle Bred, we think it best to use a single rein with a jointed snaffle bit in the beginning. The noseband on the bridle should be taken up snug but not too tightly. Some trainers also use a running martingale with young horses. You will remember we described this piece of tack in our chapter on Equipment. The martingale must soon be dispensed with, however, as martingales on the Saddle Bred are not permitted and will be counted against you if you later ride with it on the horse in the show ring. In training the young horse, however, the martingale when used, helps to keep his head in place and discourage any tendency he may have to throw his head.

Now we suggest getting some light quarter boots for his forefeet. These offer protection to the horse's quarters in case he hits himself in making a stride. The quarters are very tender and cracks in the heel are definitely hard to heal, especially in a young horse because he is so active. The hinged quarter boots are preferred. However, rubber boots to begin with are satisfactory.

From this time on, especially if you are training your horse to show, it will be very necessary for you to keep the horse "up in the bit" or collected, except during rest periods, which in the beginning should be frequent. Do not use spurs to keep him alert unless he is unusually lazy. A small twig or whip might be carried to touch him on the neck and keep him collected. When he is collected, he is alert and his head is carried high. He is also better balanced. By balance, we mean that his weight is spread more evenly over his body. Because of the weight of his head and neck, he is heavier from the mid-portion of his back forward than to the rear. Consequently, when his head is up and held high, more of his weight is distributed toward his back. This is why we strongly advocate driving him for balance, as he goes with his head in a position to give his body more perfect balance. Because you train your Saddle Bred to go "up in the bit" and collected, it makes him a more pleasant animal to ride, as he is better balanced, alert and instantly responsive to your rein.

Handle your reins lightly in training but with enough pressure

Courtesy B. F. Gustafson

FIG. 32   A two-wheeled jogging cart is commonly used in hitching and driving the young colt.

to let your horse know that you are there. This keeps him responsive.

The Cavalry, many foreign authorities and with few exceptions followers of the Thoroughbred and Half-Bred, use certain signals to the horse of hand and leg, which are known as "aids." They also use a slightly different type of flat saddle and sit a different seat. More will be said of these "aids" later; however, an "aid" is merely a method of communication or signal to your horse.

The next step in schooling is to find a straightaway, about sixty to eighty yards long, to begin working on his gaits. A slight slope is advantageous. It should be smooth and not too stony. At no time use a paved road or a road with much traffic. A country road is ideal if it does not contain deep ruts.

After you have decided when and where you are going to begin operations under saddle, put on the martingale, if you are going to use one, and the quarter boots. Walk your horse from the barn to the training ground or road that you have selected. If there is a grade to the road or training ground, start him going up hill or at the lower part. Urge him into a trot by touching him on the neck or mane with a twig, commanding him to trot or giving him a slight kick with your heels. His trot will undoubtedly be quite "sloppy" for some time. If he has been driven or longed, it will be more finished than if you started him under saddle with no previous training.

In the trot you should look for balance, elasticity, straightness of motion and flexing of the joints more noticeably than in the walk. With the Saddle Bred, especially the show type, you must develop speed with form. This is where you can appreciate the youngster's having been hitched before putting on the saddle. It is necessary that your horse have a good brisk trot.

Make sure he has plenty of hock action and his hocks are well under him as he goes. Any "spreading" or "going wide behind," which is a tendency to throw his hocks out, is objectionable. Often these faults may be curbed by corrective shoeing. Insufficient length of stride and flexing at the knees are other faults that must be corrected and different weight or type of shoe will often help. If need be, the quarter boots may be weighted to increase action in front. However, this should not be necessary in the young horse.

Toe weights increase your horse's tendency to extend and when he extends he has to go higher, which is what you want. Heel weight helps your horse to "fold" or "roll." (Notice how the knees and ankles of the finished horse bend while at the trot in Figures 3, 4, and 6.) This is why you need to use a capable shoer of your breed of horse, as he will study your horse's way of going and often correct certain faults through shoeing. It is important to watch his way of going during training so shoes may be changed from time to time. Though the Saddle Bred naturally has a tendency toward action, it must be encouraged and developed. Long toes, weighting and shoeing are important devices for doing so.

Be careful not to "over-ride" as this will cause a "hopping behind" and is not graceful. By "over-riding," we mean making the horse do more than his state of training warrants.

Keep your horse going at the trot as straight as possible but in the beginning do not worry him too much and be sure to handle his mouth lightly. When he "breaks" his gait, gently settle him down and start back on the trot again. Never go on as if it were all right for him to "break." Keep talking to him and petting him, as it gives him more confidence.

The horse will fret and lather considerably at the mouth and body for he is being subjected to something new. When you reach the upper end of the straightaway, stop and turn him around. Going back down grade use the stepping pace, which is the forerunner of the rack. In most instances the rack is much harder to teach than the trot. Be sure you are able to recognize the step and pace, slow gait and rack. However, if it is hard for you, have a friend stand back a bit from where you are training to be sure he is attempting the gait you want.

The down grade on return will facilitate the stepping movement. The pace is a fast movement in which the two feet on each side move forward simultaneously, whereas the stepping pace involves a slower stepping movement. In teaching the rack, the horse will learn from shuffling along in a stepping pace in the beginning. (See Figure 5 for illustrations of gaits.)

As you start down grade, "pick up" the reins and gently pull your horse's head from side to side in cadence with his forelegs. This is often called "shaking his head." Urge him forward by "clucking" or using a switch. The clucking will be easier as your hands will be "full of reins."

At the start be satisfied with only a few steps. Be patient, pet your horse on the neck and when he breaks, which will be often, start him over. Do not let him trot when you are on the down grade at this time. If he tries to trot, stop him immediately and take him back into the stepping pace shuffle. When you reach the end of your training stretch, then start back at the trot.

For the first few days two or three times over the training stretch will be enough for him. He is using his muscles differently than he has ever used them before and he will tire quickly. The training period may be lengthened as his muscles strengthen and he gains confidence.

In teaching the rack, some trainers recommend less toe and weight on the forefeet than on the hind feet, as a means of facilitating desired movements.

If you are training your horse in only three gaits, you will spend your time on the trot and not attempt to go into the stepping pace preparatory to the rack.

After a few days, the colt will begin to understand what is expected of him and as the days go on, your task will become easier. He will not learn it all in a week, so above all else—have patience. This same routine will have to be continued for many days. In three or four months, if his trot is square and you can count it— one, two, three, four—if his step and pace are even and if he will go the length of the runway slowly but surely without breaking, you can be very proud of him and yourself too.

If the colt you are training is three years old and sound, one day's rest a week should now be enough. However, some trainers recommend two days a week even at three years.

Your colt is not ready to canter or gallop while you are mounted. Keep him at a collected walk in going and coming from the stable and once or twice during the training period stop, dismount and allow the horse rest periods for a minute or two.

While in these rest periods, if you have not taught him before, you might teach him to "stretch" or "park" while you mount and dismount. "Parking" or "stretching" means the horse's hind and forelegs are evenly placed and the forelegs are extended a little

ahead of the natural stand. This can be overdone, so do not teach
him to stand with his legs extended out too far. It can best be
taught by holding the reins in your left hand, standing at his head
facing the rear, and touching him lightly on the rear of the ankle
with the toe of your shoe, until he will move his foot forward. Repeat the process until he will stand without moving. Do not expect
him to stand very long at first. Pet him encouragingly and soon
he will stand that way till you make him move out. (See Figure
33.) Your horse must assume this position while being judged in
the show ring, especially so if you intend showing your Saddle
Bred in model Classes.

Many horsemen will advise you against working your horse in
the same place every day. They will tell you that he will go stale
and lose interest, that you should vary his exercise ground. We do
not suggest this. After a few days of training in the same place,
he will know exactly what is expected of him. If he gets sluggish,
tap him lightly on the neck with your whip and he will respond.

As your colt begins to "get his feet under him" and will go back
and forth without breaking, start urging him to move faster. A
five-gaited horse, to be a good one, must have lots of speed at the
rack and trot. Try not to hurry him too much at one time·but
build him up gradually. With this new speed, you are now beginning to rack on one hand and developing a good sound trot on
the other. At this time you may begin to "steady his head" and
"balance him on the bit."

If your horse has been wearing a "bitting harness" part of each
day while in the stall, he will be learning to carry his head correctly. If not, you must start really working in earnest on his head
flexions at the poll. He must carry his head high, but flex enough
to bring his chin in, instead of pointing it way out in front of him,
often referred to as "star gazing."

Some trainers call steadying his head, "balancing him on the
bit." During his training process, you have been "shaking his
head" by pulling the reins from side to side in teaching him to
rack. Now as you "lift" him into the stepping pace or the slow gait
preparatory to going into the rack, as he steps out, stop shaking
his head and hold him steady. Use enough firmness to keep his step
true. You will notice that there will be a little more pull on one

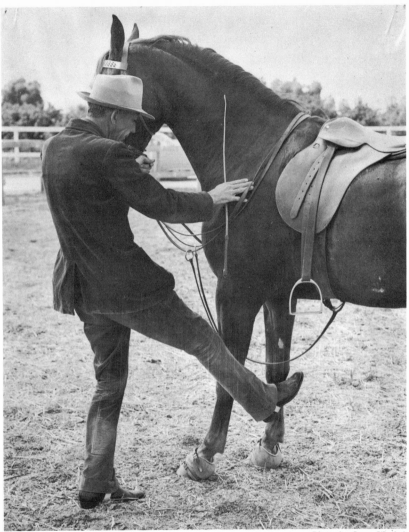

Photo by Ivan Mashek

FIG. 33   In teaching the horse to "stretch" or "park," touch the rear of his ankle or knee with the toe of your shoe making him move his forefoot forward slightly as illustrated by Jim Dickey, trainer.

rein than the other. If he should "break," slow him up and start him over in the same gait. When he is stepping along in the rack, hold him steady, balance him and he can be urged along a bit faster by clucking and talking to him.

It will not be too difficult to hold a small whip in your right hand with the reins and, if necessary, it can be used on the horse's neck or shoulder to produce the desired results. This will help to keep him collected, and with both hands handling the reins, it will be easier for you to have your mount flexed at the poll and keep his head steady.

This is the period in which you make your horse's mouth. Continue to use the same snaffle bit that you started with. Be gentle in manipulating it and you will notice how much less pressure you have to use on the reins to get the animal to answer. As the training periods progress, if you do not yank or pull unnecessarily on him, his mouth will become increasingly responsive. Constant sawing on his mouth in "shaking his head" will often cause the tender young mouth to bleed.

Up to this point your horse has learned no definite gait other than as far as he has gone with the walk, rack and trot. After he gets his "feet under him" and a fair reach, the slow gait and rack may be worked on. We do not believe that a horse who is showing good signs of progress at this stage should be allowed to rack without first being taken into the slow gait. Do not go into the slow gait from any other gait than the walk.

The slow gait must be done with precision, grace and rhythm. The horse must be highly collected and exhibit superb action. When "lifting" the horse into the slow gait, if he starts to step out too fast, gather him, hold his head up and exert enough pressure on the bit to keep him slow, with maximum action. (See Figure 34.) When you are ready to let him rack, let him have his head slightly, releasing pressure on the rein and "cluck" to him. Do not let him spread out too much, however. Keep him flexed at the poll and hold him steady. Urge him on with as much speed as possible.

Later on you will slow gait and rack him using a curb bit with a double bridle, but for the time being, keep on using the single rein snaffle.

The rack is not a natural gait with most horses. It must be developed by training and practice. It is a four beat gait, each foot striking the ground at a separate and distinct time. When executed on hard footing, it should beat a regular 1-2-3-4 sound. It should be performed with ease and grace, ample height to the stride and, like the trot, with as much speed as possible while form and action are maintained.

As your horse's walk, slow gait, rack and trot, are improving, you should begin to test your signals or aids. Up to this time you have been trotting upgrade and racking back. You have separated the slow gait and rack and are also walking him. Now, with the use of your "aids" or the signals you gave him, begin to trot him and rack him in both directions. Rack for one length and trot for two or three and vice versa. The horse is a great child of habit. He associated one way up your training road with one gait and the other direction with the other gait. Now, you and your horse must get together on the signals you give him. To assist you in this, you might work him on some other straight piece of ground close by. It is best that you trot him more often than you rack as the rack is very tiring, especially to young horses.

Be sure your horse does what you signal him to do, but do not confuse him. Do not make him responsible for your mistakes. If he is in the wrong, stop him and start over immediately. This process will take you several more days to even out.

At this time, if you have been teaching your horse to "park" while you mount and dismount, you may also begin to teach him to "back." If you are still driving one or more times each week, he should also be taught to "back" while hitched. It is imperative that he know how to back with a minimum of effort. At a show, especially in stake and professional classes, the judge will inevitably ask each rider and driver to back his horse a few steps.

To teach your mount to "back" when mounted, first have him "park," gather him, then gently take up on the reins, at the same time repeating the word BACK. You may also touch him around the elbow with the toe of your riding shoe without extracting your foot from the stirrup iron. Two or three steps are sufficient. You will find that you can keep him backing in a straight line by exerting leg pressure on either side. After you have backed him the

FIG. 34   Trainer Jim. Dickey is schooling the above horse in the slow gait.
(Note the running martingale.) He is exerting enough pressure on the reins
for the colt to carry his head high and lift up his knees.

desired distance, stop and allow him to walk up to the position from which he started backing. When he gets there, have him park again for a few seconds. In a week or so you will not have to pull him back, but just by gathering the reins and saying BACK, he will respond. A similar method can be used in teaching him to "back" while hitched. Here you will probably need an assistant at first to touch him on the knees as you pull him back with the reins.

After the horse has learned to respond to the slow gait, rack, walk and trot, continue your further training in a ring. If a ring is not available, tramp out an oval in a field or pasture by walking or longeing your horse there and he will wear down a track in a very short time. If you have a grader or rake at your disposal, you can make a path about five yards wide. The oval should be from 150 to 200 feet long and from 75 to 100 feet in width. Try to keep the ring as even as possible.

Your first few experiences with your "green" horse in the ring will undoubtedly cause you much grief all over again. Remember —your patience! You have had to use much of it up until now. In the beginning, every time he goes around the curve he will break his gaits, especially at the rack. This again will take time to smooth out. Keep him steady and slow him up a bit as he goes into the turns. The horse will gradually gain confidence and start to take the curves like a veteran show horse before you realize it. Reverse him often as he will tire and get stale going in the same direction.

Most trainers like to school their young horses in a small ring. They feel that by doing this they never need worry about the horse breaking his gait if he is ever shown later in a smaller than average size show ring. He would take the turns in a larger show ring just that much easier and faster.

Remember to keep driving your horse once or twice a week even at this stage, as driving will do wonders for his trot. Be sure not to let him do any gaits but walk and trot while in harness.

When you are satisfied that your horse is doing well with the gaits that you have taught him and with the turns in the ring, you can direct your attention to the last gait of the five-gaited American Saddle Bred horse—the canter. Do not confuse this with the gallop. It is much slower. However, in the beginning, the gallop or just plain run, is what he will want to do.

The canter is not usually difficult to learn and some horses take to it very quickly and easily.

The Saddle Bred is not whipped or driven into the canter but always urged into it from the walk and from no other gait. There are two leads, the left and the right. In teaching the canter, if you do not have a ring to work in, find a path or road along the side of a fence or rail. As your horse goes forward at a walk with his right or off side next to the fence or rail, turn his head toward the fence and shift your weight forward and to the left, using your right heel or a little leg pressure slightly back of the girth. By doing this you throw the horse enough off balance to make him reach out with his left foreleg and this will put him on the left lead when stepping out into the canter. You must then adjust your seat and hands. The lead leg will be raised higher than the other foreleg as he moves at the canter.

To put the horse on the right lead, the same method is reversed. Here is an easy way to remember whether he is on the correct lead: The lead leg should always be the leg nearest the center of the ring while you are riding next to the rail. We presume that you can recognize these leads while mounted without having to stretch forward to watch the forelegs. Watch the horse's shoulders. They will tell you.

Exercise your horse as much on one lead as on the other. Most horses have a tendency to favor one lead more than the other, but by training, this preference can be reduced until he will take one lead as readily as the other. Often, too, the horse will try to go "sideways" as in the "passage" or "two-trot" while cantering. If you cannot break him of this habit, it might become necessary to use spurs to keep his hindquarters where they belong.

It is possible that the horse may canter "false." In other words, be on the right lead with the forelegs and the left lead with the hind. It is very unnatural and you cannot help but notice it when mounted. If this should happen, stop him and start the gait over again. While training, always work or exercise your horse close to the rail. This will make him more accustomed to it as he must stay close to the rail in horse shows except when passing another horse.

The canter is a fine gait, is good to look at, easy for the horse and comfortable for the rider to sit. The stride should be of reasonable length and not too high. He should canter with ease on either lead. A reasonable amount of speed is necessary but it should not be as fast as the gallop. The things to watch in this gait are too much or not enough action, too much speed, lack of agility, promptness in starting, and hitting the ground too hard. A medium must be sought. The Cavalry divided the canter into three beats, which are the positions of the horse's legs in this gait. In slow motion you can see the drive is all from the rear quarters.

The hardest task in teaching the young horse to canter is to make him canter slowly, go collected and with lots of action. The young horse in the beginning often wants to start in an extended gallop. If unable to slow him down after a couple of weeks, you might take him into the center of the ring and attempt to canter in small circles. Start by riding in a circle and then gradually make the circle smaller, while you keep him on the proper lead. This is hard work and if he has a tendency to throw his hindquarters away from the center of the circle, use your heel or spur to keep him in line. Reverse often in order to use both leads.

The Cavalry and many park riders use aids similar to those given here for cantering. In criticizing our method some will ask, "What do you do if you want to canter and you haven't a fence to turn his head into?" In that case, we do just as they would. A horse that has been schooled by turning him into a fence will go into his canter as easily by putting him through the same maneuver for either the right or left lead without the aid of a fence. Some trainers touch the horse in the elbow with their foot in the stirrup to make him reach out with the proper leg.

Once you start to teach the horse to canter, do it every day, but keep working on the other gaits and whatever else you may have taught him. From now on work with the five gaits is repetition, over and over. You must remember that the walk must be alert, collected and the slow gait must be at a speed showing a maximum of action. The rack and trot should be balanced and fast.

The canter must be slow on both leads. Even at this point in your training, we still say—DO NOT DISCONTINUE DRIVING. We keep repeating this in hope we can impress you with its importance. Also, make certain your horse will park and back readily.

After your horse is well gaited, that is, easily goes into each of his gaits with your signals and not break, you are ready to put on a double bridle. He has been accustomed to the snaffle but now he will also have a curb bit in his mouth. The purpose is to set his head and keep him collected. By keeping him collected, with his head up and chin tucked, it facilitates action. Because you want a maximum of action at the slow gait, you will use your curb more than in other gaits. The curb bit will keep his head up and flexed whereas the snaffle gives him freedom of his head.

The double bridle will worry the horse in the beginning as he is not used to having so much in his mouth. He will tend to toss his head, run sideways and generally give you a lot of trouble. Be careful that nothing pinches him. The curb chain will perhaps need adjusting. Some horses need it tight, others loose. You will have to study your horse and find out through trial and error where it is most comfortable for him.

To set your horse's head in the double bridle, you must teach him to flex at the poll and keep his head up by using the curb bit. As he learns to work on this bit, you will use it also in keeping his gaits steady and true.

The principle of teaching him to use the curb is first to work on getting his head up where he should carry it for good balance with the snaffle. This you have been doing thus far by "lifting" up on the snaffle bit and keeping him collected in teaching the slow gait and rack. After he has learned to raise his head in response to lifting up on the snaffle bit, you can exert a little pressure on the curb at the same time you use the snaffle. You will note that pressure on the curb, at the same time you move him forward, will necessitate his flexing at the poll and tucking his chin to get relief from pressure of the bit. He therefore learns to answer the curb by flexing.

In using the curb, keep the rein always taut but not tight, so that only by lightly touching it he will respond with his head up and chin tucked. Mrs. Bud Bohall of Phoenix, Arizona, who has helped her husband train many fine horses uses the rule, "on the curb but light." Keep your horse always conscious you are there but handle the bit lightly. When he noses out too far, exert pressure gently with the curb and bring his head into position.

Not every Saddle Bred will develop a rack or trot suitable to show even at the smaller shows, but they will make good pleasure horses. If you are in doubt as to your horse's progress, have some competent horseman acquaintance come over and watch him "go." We have yet to meet a breeder or trainer who would not be glad to do this for you if your place is not too far away. There are things that might miss your eye that the experienced horseman would notice at a glance. The horse's shoes, bits or some other piece of equipment may be hindering him and the experienced trainer can tell you how to correct this immediately. Then again, this same horseman might advise you to roach the horse's mane and tail and convert him into a three-gaiter for show or for pleasure uses. If the advice does not seem sound to you, call another trainer and seek his advice. In this way you will be sure that you are doing the right thing.

Horses have been converted at all ages, if their gaits are not suitable to the class they are in. Usually, they are converted from five gaits to three, but they may also be converted from three to five. It is very often quite difficult to make the mane and tail grow in to look as full and flowing as it did prior to its being cut.

Some people are of the opinion that a three-gaited or walk-trot horse is not as good as the five-gaited. This is a fallacy! If you will notice the premium lists of the various large and small shows, you will find that the cash prizes in the stakes are the same in both classes.

The show points of the three- and five-gaited horse differ in that the three-gaited horse, to be a winner, must have an unusually fine head and long tapering neck. This fineness must run from stem to stern. The three-gaited must have exceptional action and manners, but speed is not necessary as in the case of the rack and trot of the five-gaiter. According to the judges of the American Horse Shows Association, the trot of the three-gaited American Saddle Bred should not exceed twelve miles per hour.

The three-gaited horse is often associated with a lady. Many trainers state that it takes a man to ride a five-gaited horse and a lady's light hand for the three-gaited. However, there are many excellent women riders of both three- and five-gaited horses.

The canter and the walk must be exceptionally fine in a three-gaited horse. The position of the head and the flex at the poll, perpendicular to the ground, if possible, is necessary in the three-gaited horse. The five-gaited horse is permitted a little more liberty in this respect.

Several persons have asked us how long it takes to gait a horse. The only answer we can give is: "It all depends on the aptness of the horse and the ability of the trainer." Some horses learn faster than others and some trainers can accomplish more with horses than others.

We know of a very finely bred three-year-old colt by *Mountain Peavine* that was in training with Walter Hughes at Northwind Farms at Lansing, Michigan, that was by no means ready to show. This horse had been schooled for more than a year. This is nothing against the trainer as perhaps the owner did not want the horse carried along any faster.

The duration of the preliminary training period in getting the young horse to do five distinct gaits without breaking, though not necessarily having all the speed in the world, depends largely on the aptness of the horse. It also depends on how fast the trainer wants to bring him along. To cite an example, Mr. J. T. Young of Lebanon, Tennessee, schooled a six-year-old gelding for eighteen months, mainly in the canter, before he would even show him to a prospective purchaser.

It is unquestionably easier to gait the young horse than to "make" or "make over" an older one. So in training your young horse, always keep in mind that you are planning his future.

TRAINING THE TENNESSEE WALKING HORSE

We have told you that the Tennessee Walking Horse has his own unique way of going, characterized by a long overstride, which was developed during plantation days in the Old South. He was essentially a pleasure horse when not being ridden by overseers on their daily round of duties. He would go at a comfortable gait called the running walk for hours without tiring himself or his rider. Now he is rapidly becoming a show horse. Each year the Champion Walking Horse of the World is picked and some of the finest of this breed are shown. Until 1953 this competition was staged at Shelbyville, Tennessee. That year, for the first time the championship selection was made at the Tennessee State Fair in Nashville.

The Walking Horse is schooled in three gaits, the flat-footed walk, running walk and canter, but his preliminary training is generally not nearly so long nor involved as that of the Saddle Bred.

Few Tennessee Walkers are foaled that have the running walk as a natural gait, although you may encounter one now and then who falls into it quite naturally, running beside his dam. By far the larger percentage of Walking Horses must develop the gait through vigorous training and weighting devices.

The Tennessee Walker is not saddled and ridden until two years old. Most trainers leave him alone until that time except for a brief period of handling at six months and again at the end of the first year. They claim that permitting the young foal to run with his dam in pasture helps to develop the looseness and naturalness of stride that are so important to his way of going. At six months you can slip a halter on your colt, lead him quietly and pick up his feet. This is all that is necessary until he becomes a yearling and is ready to be halter broken and is taught to lead and stand for grooming and care of his feet.

During the following spring and summer, turn him again to pasture, but remember that if you are planning to show him as a yearling in hand you will naturally need to groom him often to keep down the scurf. You should also occasionally review his lessons in leading.

In October, before your colt is two years old, you may begin serious training. First you must get him accustomed to the bit. We suggest you use a rubber or leather covered snaffle to begin with. Put it on and let him wear it while you lead him. The Walker is very adaptable and will become accustomed to the bit after a few days.

Instead of a bit, some trainers use a hackamore for control. This is a halter-like device with no bit, but a strap or nose-band that fits high across the nose. It has reins attached under the chin. When pulling the reins, the strap exerts pressure on the nose and cuts off the animal's wind or air. You get the same response as though you had a bit, but there is no danger of hurting his tender mouth.

Now, you may begin to get him used to the saddle. Put the saddle on the same way we have already suggested. Let him wear it in the box stall until he gets used to it. You may also lead him in the paddock with the saddle on. When he shows no sign of resisting it, you are ready to mount. In this speeded up procedure, we have seen some trainers tie the colt close to a wall and boost themselves up to and back down from the saddle. When the colt will allow this to be done quietly, the trainer on the next day will attempt to ride him at a walk. Some colts will take this in their stride whereas others will buck and try to throw the rider.

You may have to use spurs at this time to control your colt. With perseverance and patience, however, going only a very short distance each day, your colt will quiet down. When he does, let him do largely as he pleases at first. Let him go across the training ring or wherever he wants to until he is used to your being in the saddle. You will notice that in training the Tennessee Walker, we have gone straight from handling and leading to saddling with no bitting rig, longeing, long-reining or hitching. Consequently, saddling may be more unusual to him and he is apt to cut up somewhat.

When he is two years old, you may begin to ride him daily. Unless you are a light person, you should get a light boy to ride at this time, for his bones are still soft and over-riding may damage his legs. In conformation the Tennessee Walker should have good bones, that is large leg bones, and should be able to carry weight, but do not over-tax him at this early age.

Have him shod with light racing plates and two pads of leather. The colt's feet will be small and short at this age and the leather pads will build them up. You may pack around the frog lamb's cotton and lanolin. This protects the feet and keeps them healthier.

When you first begin riding him daily, let him choose his own gait. Feel him out and let him get used to being ridden. Then hold him in a flat-footed walk as this will be the first gait you will work on. Cluck to him and put a little pressure on his sides with your heel to urge him forward. Keep him settled down in a walk and going on the rail in your training ring. He will reach farther at a walk with his forefeet but will not go as fast as he will later on in his running walk. Your object is to keep him going straight with good reach, yet without going wide behind, paddling or winging. He should have a fast, bold, hard hitting 1-2-3-4 beat to his walk and nod his head excessively as he goes. A little toe weight now will help to square up his walk and keep him going straight.

At the same time you are working on his walk, teach him to turn, to park and later, as you go along, to back. You teach the Tennessee Walker while mounted to turn in the direction you pull the rein. You will have no difficulty with this when teaching him in the ring. He is used to a snaffle bridle and as you go on a curve in the ring at a walk, tighten the rein in the direction you travel on the curve and the horse soon learns to turn in the direction of the tightened rein. Some leg pressure back of the girth will help to keep his body straight.

Also, procedure in teaching him to back and park is the same as that for the Saddle Bred.

When you have got him going "square," at a fast flat-foot walk, which no doubt will take you several weeks, you may then urge him on into a faster speed. You are now beginning the most difficult part of your training, the running walk.

When he is first allowed to move on faster, he will want to go faster than a running walk. Some colts will want to pace, others to trot. It will be easier for you if he wants to pace for it is easier to develop overstride and gliding motion from the pace. The running walk is a sliding gait.

Your problem now is to move your horse from the flat-footed walk into the running walk without letting him break over into a pace or trot. Urge him forward gently until his head is swinging up and down like a pendulum and he is gliding along swiftly, with the hind feet overstepping the print of the forefeet. (See Figure 7 for illustration of the running walk.) He is now in the gait you want. If he breaks into a pace or trot, settle him down immediately and make him start over at the flat-foot walk. Then urge him along again at the running walk. To keep him going you may use a riding whip or touch him smartly with your heel in the side. Pick up your reins to "lift" his forefeet off the ground to get more action and overstride. Keep steady, but do not use heavy pressure on the bit. As he increases his speed in the running walk, he will also increase his stride and overreach.

Now you are going to strive for high action in front with a long reach and as much speed as possible. The hind feet must be carried low to the ground in a walk, overstepping the print made by the forefeet. Thus, as your colt reaches higher and farther with his forefeet, his hind feet will overstep a greater distance.

To aid you in developing this gait and to counteract any tendency to shuffle pace, you may put light chains and boots on his forefeet. Some trainers use trotting balls in the beginning and as training progresses, they use heavier chains. The horse not being used to the weight of the chains, will try to step out of them, thus picking his forefeet up higher with more action and greater length of stride.

At this point in training the weighted boot will also help to increase action. We suggest a walking horse boot. There are many tricks of the trade and we know one trainer that even blindfolds the young colt to encourage him to reach farther and higher.

One fine method for developing his running walk is to ride him over a plowed field. This will encourage him to reach. Riding him over a field of broomsage is also a particularly good way to deter any tendency to pace.

As we have pointed out, weighting devices are of utmost importance in his training, particularly when he is not a natural Walker. Therefore it is imperative that your farrier be accustomed to shoeing the Tennessee Walker and know how to improve his way of going. Generally, if your colt is a pacer type you must raise his heel and pad and extend the toe. If a trotter type, lower his heel and pad and extend the toe. The toe weight is for forward motion and stride, whereas heel weight is for higher knee action. As the colt's foot grows, heavier shoes are used. Shoe weight for this breed when trained for show, generally runs 16 to 36 ounces.

As you go along with developing the running walk, be sure that your colt is walking. Getting speed in the running walk is dangerous, for your horse is apt to be doing some mixed up gait rather than the running walk. An average true running walk overreach with training today is 36 inches though some go up to 60. An occasional trainer will say that he has his going 70 to 100 inches but it is doubtful if they are really walking.

The colt's motion in his running walk comes from the shoulders. He will nod his head in cadence with his stride. You can be sure that if his head is not nodding, he is not in the running walk. While you are working on gaits in the beginning you need not worry too much about his head carriage. It will no doubt be quite low.

After he is well along in the flat-foot walk and running walk, which will probably take several weeks, you may begin to work on his head. The Walking Horse is more relaxed in his way of going and is not highly collected as is the Saddle Bred, though he is trained to be responsive and alert.

You get your horse's head up through his mouth and reins. Put a low port curb bit on him with a loose chin strap. He wears only a single bridle with the curb. Tighten the chin strap as he gets used to it, and hold your hands higher giving shorter rein. This will raise his head. The tighter you keep the reins, the higher he will hold his head. You want him to carry his head high but with his chin slightly extended. If you give him too short a rein, so that his head is cramped, he gets too "trappy," that is he shortens his strides and will either nose out or tuck his nose. You do not want him geared up and high strung, yet you want him responsive and paying attention to his business.

To get more motion with his head, use a swivel bit, flexible to port. After his mouth becomes responsive to your signals, you can put on a higher curb bit. The Walking Horse bit generally used is a long shank bit with curved cheeks. The long shank gives you leverage, which helps you collect your horse, keep his head up and keep his gaits true. Some trainers use seven inch shanks, some nine inch. Select your Walking Horse bit and the length shank to fit your individual horse. If he has a tendency to carry his head too low, a very long shank will help bring it up. If he persists in getting his head too high and tends to nose out, use a standing martingale to hold his head down in training.

Your job during your colt's second year is repetition and more repetition to perfect his walk and running walk. Though speed is the object of the professional trainer today, for you as an amateur it may be disastrous. You may not be able to recognize a break from the running walk into a stepping pace. In both gaits the animal overreaches but you will notice a difference in the feel of the ride.

At the stepping pace you feel a sidewise motion in the saddle, whereas at the running walk, you are almost motionless. That is why the gait is so comfortable to ride. If there is any motion at all, you will feel it as a forward and backward motion. Also remember that for your horse to be walking his head must be nodding straight like a pendulum. He will also flick his ears and chomp on his bit.

If you have got him going well in his gaits, you may show him during the summer of his second year. If he looks like a good show prospect, you may want to have his tail set during the spring. The Walker is generally shown with his long flowing tail carried high.

In the fall, shortly before he is three years old, you may begin to teach him the canter. Do this just as we have already suggested with the Saddle Bred. Getting him to use the correct lead may be taught by a slightly different method. If the left lead is desired, shift your weight forward and to the left and touch him on the left shoulder with the toe of your shoe. When going in a small circle at this gait he will reach out with his correct lead to keep his balance.

After your horse has learned the signals for going into a canter on both leads, you will endeavor to make this gait slow and rolling. The horse will want to go fast, perhaps into a gallop, but you must keep it slow. This is a matter of keeping him collected through rein pressure. Some trainers find an upgrade good for teaching the canter as it tends to keep the horse slower. Also, as we suggested with the Saddle Bred, cantering him in a small circle will help him to slow down and put him on the correct lead. By keeping him turning by rein pressure to the left, he keeps going on his left lead in a circle. To change to the right lead, shift to the right touching the toe of your right foot into his shoulder as you circle him to the right. He will reach out on the right lead. And likewise he will circle to the right rein pressure from that side. Later he will come to associate shifting of your weight with going into the canter.

From now on your work is merely repetition of work on his gaits. Judges in the ring today want speed and overstride. Let us caution you again, however, to be careful with speed at the running walk and always warm him up from the walk before going into this gait.

TRAINING THE HUNTER AND JUMPER

Hunting is one of our oldest sports. Horse and man have been an inseparable team in this thrilling diversion of following hounds across open fields and through wooded glens on the trail of an elusive quarry. Consequently, it is no wonder that countless books have been written on developing mounts of great courage and daring who can negotiate any obstacle they encounter.

Because of this wealth of information that is already in print, we will not attempt to deal with the details of producing a hunter or jumper. Instead we will limit ourself to the broader general principles that will acquaint you with the training.

The Thoroughbred is commonly used as a hunter or jumper, for he has the indispensable characteristics of being spirited and high strung. It is this endowment of nervous energy that keeps him going ever onward, never faltering, to the last mile of a long, hard hunt. Some people say a Half-Bred will give up when he gets too tired, but never the Thoroughbred. Many Half-Bred owners will strongly dispute this, saying their Half-Breds will go equally as far and as pleasantly. On the whole, capable Thoroughbreds have great heart, will to do, power and stamina. They out-class the Half-Bred in conformation and looks.

In selecting a hunter, you will want a sure-footed mount that is strong, willing and able to gallop for miles in the course of a hunt. You want him quiet, safe, mannerly and easily controlled around other horses or hounds. A good hunter will enjoy the hounds and hunt as much as you. You want an animal that will go wherever you direct and jump whatever you confront him with. He should be able to move on at any pace you set without your having to repeatedly slow him down or increase his speed. You want him to give you a comfortable ride, go into his fences straight, without ducking or hesitating. He must be able to carry your weight.

You should not start training your hunter or jumper before he is two years old, and then not under saddle until almost three. Your serious training should not commence until he is three. The young horse will have the stamina and energy to go, but training that is too early may result in spavins and splints. It is also a strain on a young horse to jump anything over three feet.

Begin the training of your hunter or jumper very carefully. You must be certain never to frighten him and to make him obedient and safe. He must develop complete confidence in you. These points are a necessity for a safe hunter. Three-quarters of an hour a day is enough to work a young horse.

Some trainers begin as we do with the Saddle Bred by letting the young horse stand in the stall with a "bitting rig" on to set his head and to get him to flex at the poll. Others either do not use a "bitting rig" at all or not until later in training, as they say it is impossible to know where to set his head in the beginning. You do not know where he will carry it. Morton W. (Cappy) Smith of Middleburg, Virginia, who is well known for his success, does not use a "bitting rig" until after he has the horse performing on the longe and in long-lines. Other prominent horsemen do not suggest using this tack. They teach the horse gradually to raise his head by accepting support of his bit with lightly increased tension of the reins.

In moving across country a hunter carries his head naturally, and extended forward so that he can see where he is going and judge safe footing. On approaching jumps and in the show ring, his head is carried higher and he is more collected. He must judge his take off over each obstacle and the position of his head helps him to judge his approach and to give him balance in jumping.

It is suggested that to achieve naturally good head carriage, begin with mounted training. Encourage the horse at first to carry his head and neck as natural for him. As he is ridden and maintains a constant light contact with the bit, he will gradually stiffen his neck and raise his head. Be careful not to apply too heavy tension on the reins or he will tend to arch his neck. Work him at a walk.

As the training progresses, the aim is to get relaxation of the lower jaw muscles so that when you apply continued stronger tension of the reins, his mouth will open slightly. Thus, with relaxation of the jaw, increased tension of the reins will be accompanied by some bending of the neck and flexing at the poll.

Brig. Gen. Harry D. Chamberlin suggests that with this method for getting collection and greater elevation of the head, the trainer must begin to use his legs strongly. Compel greater impulsion forward and at the same time use some restraint by tightening the reins. With this restraining force and being trained to relax his jaw and flex at the poll, the horse will further raise his neck and bring his hocks underneath him. Impulsion for jumping is also strengthened. He suggests demanding the horse to move out readily from a halt, and increases of speed at the trot.

Trainers of the Thoroughbred, often first acquaint the young horse with the mouthing bit. This is a straight barred snaffle with a ring in the center, containing another small ring with three tiny beads or "players." The colt plays with these beads in his mouth while standing in the stall. Do not let him play with the bit long at a time. You can as easily start off with letting the colt wear the snaffle bit after he is gentled. A good time to let him wear it is during the course of his feeding. Adjust it loosely so that he will not resist it.

Serious training should begin with teaching your horse to obey you on the longe.

For longeing, put on a breaking cavesson, which is similar to a halter but has a wide metal noseband with a ring in the center where you can attach the longe. If you don't have a cavesson, a rope halter with your rope line attached may have to suffice. Teach the horse to go on the longe to your commands just as we have described in training the Saddle Bred. With the hunter and jumper, however, you will need to spend several weeks in this phase of his training. In addition to exercise and balance, you are making him completely obedient to you.

It is also good to free-longe him, that is teach him to go in the ring to your commands without being on the line. This further develops your control. You will need to have him well schooled and obedient on the longe before you attempt this. Start him in a small enclosed ring so that it will be easier for him to obey you. We have seen some trainers make such a ring by using ropes stretched between buildings or fences in the paddock area. You stand in the center with a whip just as you have done when you held the line. Command your horse to walk, trot, canter, turn and whoa, just as you have done with the longe line. The hunter, however, is taught to turn only to the inside of the circle or ring.

After several weeks of longeing, if you have him well under control, begin training him in long-lines. You must be careful not to pull on the horse's mouth in the beginning as this is very easy to do. Some trainers use a hackamore at first and as the horse learns, they put on a snaffle. However, if you are going to start out with a snaffle, you may find it useful to use what is called a ring artillery snaffle. It has large rings on either side of the mouth and prevents the bit from slipping through.

Attach the inside line to the ring of your snaffle. Then attach the outside line to the snaffle on the off-side and bring it through the ring of the surcingle, which is a strap that fits around his body at the girth. Then bring the line alongside his body.

To go in a curve or a circle, the trainer pulls slightly on the inside rein that runs directly to his hand and the horse will turn his head slightly in that direction. The rein that follows alongside his body on the off-side side helps keep his body straight. The technique is for the trainer, whose position is behind the horse, to step just to the inside of the circle and guide him as he goes in a circle by tightening the inside rein slightly and letting the off-side rein that he is holding hang loosely around the hind quarters of the horse. Heretofore he has been responding only to voice commands. Now you are beginning to guide him with the reins. You will need a helper to lead him at first.

When he has learned to travel correctly in a circle in both directions, you may then slip the inside rein also through the ring of the surcingle. Now you will drive him in straight lines and turns between the reins on both sides of him. This makes it easier to keep his body straight.

FIG. 35   You may begin jump training by longeing the horse over a pole on the ground, as demonstrated here. Notice that the pole is painted to attract the horse's attention.

FIG. 36   When the horse has learned to step over the obstacle at the walk, he will hop over it when longed at a trot.

Trainers will sometimes drive a horse five and six miles at a walk and slow trot. Driving your colt will help get his hocks well under him. This is important for his way of going and for jumping. Even long after your horse is a seasoned jumper, you will find driving in long-lines good exercise and discipline. Dr. Lew Llewalyn of Auburn, Alabama, says that when his finished jumpers get sloppy in their jumps and try to refuse, that he works them very hard in long-lines for several days. He says that he never has a jumper refuse in the show ring.

When you have mannered your colt with long preliminary training and he will answer to your voice commands and to reins, you may introduce him to the saddle and mount as we have already advised. This should take you up to the fall before he is three years old.

Most trainers we know begin the colt's jumping education along with his general education. Of course it is very simple jumping and involves no height.

Begin your colt's jump training in the ring or on a straightaway. Lay on the ground either a pole or log which is no more than twelve inches thick. The horse is more apt to notice an object of this height. At first, lead him over the obstacle at a walk. Then lead him in the opposite direction again walking over it. After you have done this several times and the horse shows no reluctance to stepping over the pole, you can begin to longe him over it. If he should refuse while on the longe, lead him over it again. Permit him to stop and look the obstacle over if he shows any fear of it. Teach him, however, that he must go forward and over it.

Longe him only at a walk. When he will take the pole in his stride, you can then increase his pace to a slow trot. When he comes to the pole he is almost certain to jump over it. If he doesn't, lead him over it again. When he does jump over it, pet him to show that he has performed correctly.

We have pointed out to you before and want to emphasize again that there are variations in training method and nearly every trainer will work differently. The greatest reason for difference will probably lie with the horse. No two horses are alike, hence training has to be varied to meet the needs of the horse.

A rather different and interesting method of teaching the young horse to jump, which is commonly used in the West, is illustrated in Figures 37, 38, 39, 40, and 41. We have watched Mr. Bud Landrum, trainer, at the Colin Campbell Ranch in Phoenix, Arizona, use this procedure very effectively. In the beginning the trainer teaches the horse to turn and answer to voice commands in long-lines. (Known as ground driving in the West.) At the same time he also teaches the colt to jump. The longe line attached is somewhat different from what we have heretofore described. He takes a rope about 30 feet long and makes a halter-like contraption to fit over the horse's head. This device is made so that a pull on the rope will exert pressure on all the tender nerve areas around his head.

It is made by first tying a small slip-knot on the end of the rope. By running the opposite end of the rope through the slip-knot, it will form a loop or noose which you will place around the horse's neck. With the free end of your rope, reach down with your left hand about three feet below the horse's throat, and make another loop or circle about one foot in diameter by grasping the rope and turning your hand over and where the loop meets, grasp with your right hand. Then reach farther down on the rope with your left hand and bring a small loop through the large loop you are holding in your right hand. Take the part you are holding in your left hand, which is the small loop, and place it over the poll and behind the horse's ears. Adjust the part you are holding with your right hand around his nose and over his chin. Then the free end of the rope will come out right over his left cheek bone and is like a pulley. When you pull the rope, there is pressure on top of his head, on his nose and on both chin bones, all the vulnerable nerve spots. The device will cause him to obey instantly.

The device is commonly used in the West and horses are taught to jump with it on. The horse is first led over the jump so that he will understand what to do. He is then worked over the jump on the rope. He is not worked in a circle or ring at this time.

Trainers using this method believe in starting the horse over jumps much higher than we have suggested, at two and one-half feet. We observed however a very quiet youngster, trained in this

Photo by Ivan Mashek

FIG. 37   Bud Landrum, trainer, demonstrates how the longe rope is looped
around the horse's head. Take the part you are holding in your left hand and
place it over the poll and behind the horse's ears.

Fig. 38   Work quietly as you slip the rope over his head.

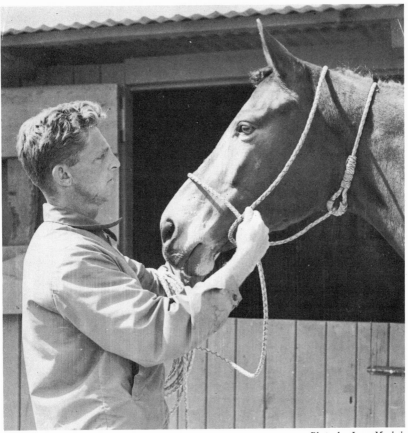

FIG. 39 Adjust the part you are holding with your right hand around his nose and over his chin.

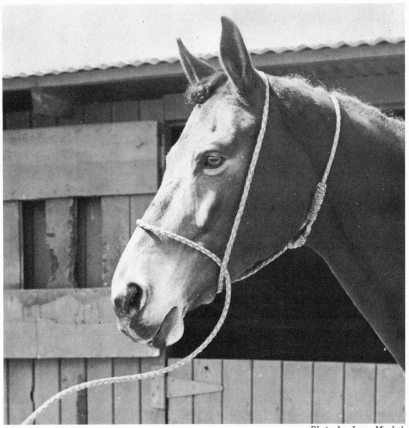

Photo by Ivan Mashek

Fig. 40 Notice how the rope touches on the chin bones, nose and top of head. When it is pulled, pressure is exerted on all three areas.

Photo by Ivan Mashek

FIG. 41   The trainer demonstrates teaching the young horse to jump over an obstacle 3 feet high. The rope is used as a longe. If the horse refuses to jump, a pull on the rope will make him instantly respond. This trainer finds it particularly useful if he is training a stubborn horse.

way, clear three and one-half foot fences when he had not jumped more than 20 obstacles previously. An objection to this method of teaching a hunter might be the difficulty you would encounter in teaching him good jumping form. Great care must be taken in early training to make the horse completely obedient to you. This must be done by gradually giving him new things to do and being careful never to frighten him. This is especially necessary to make your colt safe in jumping.

In using the method we first described, which is more generally used, and your horse is jumping the twelve inch obstacle without difficulty, you can raise the jump gradually one to two inches at the time. When you reach two feet, begin to include two or three other jumps in the ring of the same height. It is good to have three in a row so the horse will only have time to land and jump again.

After your horse has progressed enough to be mounted and is three years old, begin working on his gaits in earnest. You may have him shod with light three ounce plates. If he is being trained in stony country and you are hacking him about the country in working on his gaits, cover his feet with leather pads. It is hard for horses to jump on hard ground and the pads offer a lot of protection. His feet should be round without much toe, with only a low heel and almost level with the ground. "Jar calks" are often placed diagonally on each side of the forefoot shoe to dig into the ground preventing the horse from slipping, and to absorb some of the jar in jumping. The hind feet may be shod with a heel on one side and feathered on the other. We know one trainer who has his hunters shod behind with one-quarter inch block heels, and he works them for about three weeks in their gaits with no shoes on their forefeet. He does this because it makes the forefeet tender and a young horse is then easier to quiet down. Also he finds it a good way to get the horse's hocks under him and to gain better balance, because you want more of his weight on the hindquarters. In addition, if the horse is inclined to step on himself in going, it is best to have no heel on the inside of his hind feet.

For mounted schooling, some trainers use either a standing or a running martingale. The martingale may be worn in shows by these horses without it counting against them. It gives more control and is useful on an untrained horse.

Here's how to tell whether a standing martingale is correctly adjusted: If the strap from the chin follows the contour of the horse's head and runs easily up under the point of the neck, it is properly adjusted. It will now give ample freedom for his head. If it won't reach this high, it is too tight and won't allow the freedom needed in jumping.

Continue to use a snaffle bit in working your horse in his gaits. Begin with his walk. You may command him to walk and give him the rein slightly as you have done in longeing and long-reining him. Now, at the same time, begin to use the riding "aid" of squeezing your legs slightly to move him forward in a walk. He will later associate only the pressure of your legs and the slight give of the rein with moving out at a walk.

You want him to go in a well-extended, free walk, putting each foot down hard as he takes a natural stride. He must go straight with his hocks well under him. He should not throw his legs to either side.

You doubtless will have to work a lot on his trot. The Thoroughbred is not a natural trotter and you will have to concentrate on getting it extended. The horse may want to go in a choppy, short stride. You do not want any squaring or reaching up with action in his trot. It is good to trot him frequently in long-lines.

You may use the same method we have already told you about to teach him to canter when mounted. As you go into your left lead, shift your weight forward and to the left and exert leg pressure behind the girth with your right leg. Later on the horse will associate only the shift in weight. After your horse has learned his gaits and can respond to your elementary signals, you will want to work on increasing and decreasing his speed such as from the canter to a gallop. If you plan to show him as a hunter hack and bridle path hack, he will need schooling in a collected gallop. The judge will then want him flexed at the poll and up in the bridle.

Smooth increase and decrease of speed in your hunter is absolutely essential for the show ring as well as the hunting field. You may want to move out quickly at a gallop while on a hunt and stop equally as quickly when there is sudden danger. Therefore a good hunter must be trained to answer you, but not have to be prodded on or constantly slowed down. He should go at a good hunting pace, be responsive and able to change his actions at the slightest signal.

To stop your horse with your aids, tighten the reins and lean slightly backwards with your legs closed around your horse.

It ordinarily takes a professional about three months to get him going in his gaits. No doubt it will take you longer. It is a good idea then to hack him about the countryside. Horses that have been raised in the average pasture and barnyard, especially where there is other stock, are used to sights and sounds by the time they are three years old. If your horse is not quiet, however, you will have to proceed slowly and bring him in contact with noises and objects of various kinds.

After your horse is safe around noises and different sights, begin to hack him over country roads, pastures and trails in the woods. It is good to have dogs around also.

At this time many trainers begin using a curb bit, others continue with a snaffle. You want to keep your horse's mouth light, but an untrained horse across country is safer with a curb and martingale. A pelham bit is commonly used in hunting as it combines the curb and snaffle.

The curb bit should fit at a 45 degree angle from the mouth. If it is straighter, it is too tight and is uncomfortable for your horse. In the West some trainers begin by using a little Western bit with port and roller. Before using it, however, the animal is "checked up" in the stall several days, that is he wears the bit with a "bitting rig." If you have never used a "bitting rig" in training we would not suggest using this. After your horse is "made," you may no doubt have to change his bitting from time to time.

We would not suggest mounted jumping until your horse is well along in his gaits, possibly for three months, and is jumping two to three feet on the longe. Keep longeing him over his jumps until this time, and then begin teaching him to jump mounted on jump schooling days. In training use rubber bell boots when he is jumping.

To begin your mounted jumping, we would go back to the twelve inch pole and walk him over it while leading him. Then ride him over at a walk. When he takes no notice of it, then increase his speed to a trot and go over it mounted. He will doubtless give you no trouble as he is accustomed to going over the obstacle on the longe.

After he is far enough along so that you have been hacking him about the country and he is able to take small hurdles mounted, you should begin to present him with different kinds of jumps. Prepare some brush jumps, small fences, brightly painted oil drums, sandbags or anything to give height and variety. Also prepare jumps with width and take him over narrow ditches. You can even simulate water jumps by laying blue paper in front of a brush jump and lining the edge with a pole. As your horse learns, his jumps should be gradually raised in height. As they approach three feet, you may begin to canter him into jumps. We have told you before that in the canter, the drive is from the hind legs. Consequently, this is a better gait to jump from than the trot, as it gives the horse more power.

When the horse will take these various jumps in the ring, you can begin to gallop him across the pastures in working him in his gaits and jump him at a canter over small fences and ditches that he encounters. Do not put him over any jumps that are higher than he has been jumping in the training area. Have him jumping fences, rock walls, chicken coops and small ditches in different directions. In general, prepare him for the terrain and obstacles he will meet on a hunt.

As his training progresses, you can continue to raise the jumps. A three-year-old should not be asked to jump higher than three and one-half feet.

During your jump training, you should be mindful of the way your hunter goes into his jumps and his form as he goes over the obstacle. From the first of your mounted jumping, keep your horse at attention, with his mind on his business. He will have to judge his take off and as he practices, he will become more proficient. His take off is generally as far from the jump as the obstacle is high, or a little farther. Thus in jumping a three foot fence, his take off would be about three and a half feet from the fence.

A. Standard and Bars.

B. Chicken Coop.

C. Brush Jump.

D. Fence.

FIG. 42 Types of Jumps.

E. Brick Wall.

F. Pen Jump.

G. Triple Bars
(The Hog-Back is similar with the center bar being the highest.)

H. Natural Rail Fence.

FIG. 42   Types of Jumps.

Jumping authorities will advise you to keep him collected and intent on making his jumps, but as he goes over the jump, give him his head. This means give him free rein so that he has freedom of his head as he goes over. His head will be well extended and lowered on going over to achieve balance and so that he can see where he is landing. You want his forelegs up under him with plenty of fold at the knees. His hocks should also be well under him. Notice the jumping form of the finished hunter (not the rider) illustrated in Figure 14.

Train him to go into his jumps straight, without ducking, and keep an even pace as he approaches them. As his training progresses, gallop him at a hunting pace into his jumps. Train him to take them in stride and after landing to keep right on galloping. Hacking him in the country and jumping various fences and other objects he meets will help in this respect.

If you are training an open jumper, you will not have to work him in fields, wooded areas and open country to simulate the hunting area, nor will you need to prepare jumps altogether the same as those you meet on a hunt. Your aim is to get the horse over the jump without touching it. You will not be concerned with his form in jumping but his ability to get over the jump.

Teach your jumper to go over spread jumps such as the double oxer, triple bars and hog back in addition to fences and standards with poles. (See Figure 42 for different kinds of jumps.) At this stage of training his jumps will be no higher than we suggested for the hunter, but he must be trained not to touch the obstacle.

Now back to the hunter. Along in October when he is three years old and you have given him some schooling over the countryside, you may take the young horse out to cubbing meets to introduce him to hounds and the hunt. At this stage your horse will be very, very green and you must not let him get too close to other horses. Stand apart from the others and let him see the hounds and look the situation over. Horses like to run with their own kind and it might be disastrous for you to get crowded in with other horses and have your horse become excited and lose his head. At this time you are teaching him to be obedient to you and not pay attention to the other horses. You must work hard on teaching him to answer you. Stay out of the path of other horses so that they won't gallop up behind you or cut in too close to you.

You are probably not far enough along with your mounted jumping to take any obstacles at this time. You are mainly out to let your horse see the hounds, hear the horn and see a little of what is happening. As the hunting season comes on and you have had your horse out several times at cubbing meets, you may begin to bring him in closer to the hunt field. You may also be able to jump some and to gallop on occasionally in the course of the hunt. Still, watch getting too close to other horses and stay out of their path until your horse is better trained as the season progresses.

When the season is over, it is best to rest him for a few months. Also pull his shoes off. However, if you are showing him, the length of his rest period will be governed by the show season.

After your horse is four years old, his training has continued in the ring and he has hunted a season, his jumps should be gradually raised up to four feet and six inches. He should now be able to take spread jumps up to six feet. Show rules do not allow the hunter to jump above four feet and six inches; however, there is no limit to the height of jumps for the jumper. Train your horse to jump every kind of obstacle he will meet in the show ring.

One particularly fine trainer of jumpers has all of his schooling jumps outside the ring. He brings the horse into the ring and spends some little time at the walk, trot and canter on both leads. He is especially careful to keep him at a walk a large part of the time. He then goes over his school jumps, a total of five, two times and then returns the horse to the ring for more walking and work on his gaits. He has found this method to be useful as the horse associates his exercise with the quietness of his work in the ring rather than the excitement of jumping.

From now on your task is repetition and practice, with your horse becoming more proficient. Your hunter becomes better with each season he is hunted. It takes three seasons of hunting to make a seasoned hunter.

TRAINING THE WESTERN TYPE HORSE

A Western type horse is any horse skilled in the arts of the Western range and ridden under Western saddle. He can be a

Quarter Horse, Arab, Palomino, Appaloosa, Morgan, Thoroughbred or horse of mixed origin. The only requirement is that he
be trained for the role we will discuss here.

The Quarter Horse has been most commonly associated with
this type work, but Thoroughbreds are being shown with increasing frequency in stock horse classes where the Quarter Horse
had reigned supreme in the past.

For show purposes, Thoroughbred stock horses have performed
splendidly. But in actual work on the range some feel they are
too high strung to work as well as the Quarter Horse or some
other breed. The Quarter Horse is particularly useful because
of his short strides, quick getaway and ability to almost turn on a
dime.

Western horses are classified according to usage, such as the
pleasure horse, trail horse, cutting horse (cuts cattle from herd),
roping horse (used in roping cattle) and bulldogging horse (ro-
deo work). For our purpose, we will be concerned only with the
pleasure horse, trail horse and stock horse for show.

Theories vary slightly as to when you should begin a Western
horse's education, but they seem to generally agree that he can
be gentled and given some very elementary work when six months
or a year old. Actual training, however, will not begin before he
is two and one-half years of age, if a large colt, or three years if
smaller size.

When the colt is brought into the barn as a yearling for the
period of handling, and to be fed grain, most Western trainers
have a light boy under 100 pounds mount and ride. This gets
him used to the saddle. He will never forget this early handling
and will be more amenable to your will from then on.

After this stage of development, and before your more serious
work begins, there are a few lessons for you to learn.

First, don't coddle your horse. Handle him kindly, pet him
when he responds to what you ask, but always be firm. Let him
know that you will not hurt him and you do not fear him. A young
colt often cuts up because of fear that he will be hurt.

Then again, he may be equally as obnoxious when he wants to
be stubborn. A long time Arizona rancher once told us of a young
girl training her own horse, who had not been firm enough to

command obedience. The colt would lie down when she was ready to work him. She had him checked by a veterinarian, thinking perhaps he was ill. When nothing was found wrong, the trainer told her he was just being stubborn.

The next time she started to work him and he laid down, she gave him a good thrashing with her rope. The colt got up, began to work and has worked since.

Second, never feed sugar or carrots by hand as a reward. Always feed from his feed bucket. If you hand out sugar, he will grow to expect it and is apt to bite you when you don't have it.

Finally, it would be best for you to decide very early whether you want to give your colt the simple rudiments of an education and ride him for pleasure, or whether you want him to have a more finished education that will qualify him for show work. We think you will find the more advanced work will make a more enjoyable animal of him, whether you show him or not. You will more than likely want to show your horse.

Begin your training of the Western type horse just as you have other breeds. We suggest you start him on the longe with a snaffle bit, drive him in long-lines and even hitch him if you have the equipment.

"Check him up" in the beginning as you have done with other horses. The "bitting rig" Westerners use, however, is generally one improvised with a rope. They take an ordinary rope with a snap on the end and attach it to the cincha ring, run it up through the ring of the snaffle bit and secure it around the rear of the saddle letting it run in a similar pattern on the opposite side. (See Figure 43.) Do not check his head too high in the beginning and always see that he can flex more at the poll. He may wear the "rig" in the stall and during his training on the longe.

Some trainers of the stock horse will tie his head to his tail in the beginning, as it teaches him that when the rein is pulled on that side that he must come that way. This is important as we shall see later on in teaching him to turn short.

The Western type horse is also "whipped trained" to come to you very early. This is accomplished by getting him into a corner of the training area. When you command COME HERE, strike him on the rump with the whip. Being in a corner, he will have

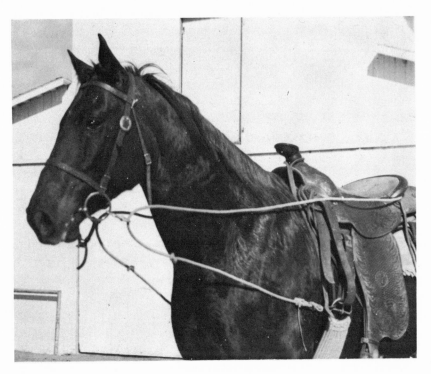

FIG. 43   A "bitting rig" on the Western type horse improvised from a rope
attached to the saddle and girth.

FIG. 44   The above amateur is training her own stock horse. She ropes off
a small ring with the aid of the barn and fence and schools her horse to
circle her free of the longe, answering her commands. When she finishes each
lesson, she commands him to COME HERE to the center of the ring.

to turn and will face you. He begins to associate COME HERE with coming toward you. He is taught this early in his training as it makes him easier to catch and more obedient.

When he is able to answer your commands on the longe and come to you, teach him to go free of the longe. (See Figure 44.)

Spend a lot of time driving him in long-lines and turning him. After you have progressed to mounted training, it is wise to free-longe him in the ring for about fifteen minutes during the first part of his lesson period.

Under saddle teach him to walk forward on command as you simultaneously lean forward. Also give with the rein and tap him with your heel. Keep him at a walk and stop him often. To stop, lean backwards with a pull on the reins as you command WHOA. Spend a lot of time at the walk in turning and doing figure eights. Figure eights get him used to turning and also to reins about his neck. As he turns, lean in the direction you want him to turn. He will begin to associate this with turning.

At this stage of his training you will teach him to go in the direction that the rein is pulled. Just as with other horses we have dealt with, you will want him to keep his body and neck straight in turning, with his head turned slightly in the direction he is going on a curve. A horse always moves away from pressure, consequently, pressing your leg behind the girth on the opposite side from which you want him to turn will help you keep his haunches straight in turning. By use of your legs you can teach him to turn his whole body and not just his head when answering the rein.

After you have worked him a good long time in his walk while mounted, have taught him to turn easily, stop and "come here" and he is used to a "bitting rig," then begin to work on his trot. Use a straightaway area to begin with, rather than a ring. Urge him into a trot by voice command, by clucking and increased pressure with the calves of your legs. You do not post to the trot in riding Western saddle.

When he has learned to answer you in the trot and you can keep him going with firmer leg pressure, work on controlling his speed. Teach him to go at a slow easy trot called a jog trot. Further emphasis is placed on stopping short and easily. Using a hackamore you can pull the reins quite firmly to stop him quickly at a trot.

Thus far in training you have used only a snaffle or a hacka-more. The hackamore is used in training as it does not harden his mouth. (See Figure 45.) When your horse is going straight in the trot and answering your signals, you are ready to work on his canter. We would not start to canter before he is approaching three years of age, if you started training at two.

The Western type horse seems to take to the canter or lope very quickly. He is taught to go into the left lead by shifting your weight forward and to the left and reining him to the left in small circles. Just the opposite is done for the right lead. When going in small circles, he has to take the correct lead to keep his balance. Change his direction in the ring so that he will go as easily in one lead as the other. When he is well along in changing leads in the ring, teach him to go in figure eights and change leads at the center of the eight. Take him into the lope only from the walk. Keep it smooth.

The Western type horse must be able to back at least 10 to 15 feet in a straight line for show. This is particularly required of the stock horse. Do this as we have told you with other breeds. Most trainers use either a snaffle bit or a hackamore for this training. Do not exert a steady pull on the reins to move him back but small pulls. Backing beside a fence will help to keep him straight as well as using pressure with your legs. Trainers of the stock horse often train and finish him in backing after he is using a bridle and curb bit. (Notice the trainer in Figure 46 teaching the young horse to back using a bridle.)

All through his training teach him not to fear ropes. While he is resting during the training period, spin a rope over his head, around his quarters and even slide it over his body.

When he has been trained to go into his gaits, to stop and turn easily and back, he can then be taught to use a mild Western curb bit if you are training him for pleasure. If you are training him as a stock horse for show, he will not use the bridle for some time yet. It generally takes at least a year to teach the fundamentals of stock horse arts before he should be bridled and finished.

A bosal hackamore is used to teach your horse to use a curb.

Fig. 45　A Hackamore as used in training and riding the Western type horse.

Courtesy Bud Landrum
Photo by Ivan Mashek

FIG. 46   Bud Landrum, trainer, teaching the young horse with his bridle on to back slowly.

This type of hackamore is made of plaited rawhide or horse hair. It has a little smaller nose piece than the regular hackamore. Be sure that the hackamore or nose piece is not too low or too high on the nose so that pressure will be applied on the chin bones. Teach him that when his head is up and he is flexed at the poll, you release the pressure on the bosal reins. Thus you release the pressure on his chin bones. Flexing his head will not be new to him as he has been wearing the "bitting rig" in training.

When you can get him to go collected in the bosal, you then put the bridle and curb bit on with it. After he has worn the bit for some time, you may start to put pressure on the bit at the same time you do on the bosal. As time goes on, substitute more pressure on the curb and less on the bosal. Finally when you are bringing no pressure to bear on the bosal, you can remove it and use the curb altogether. We suggest your starting with a mild curb as it is difficult to have light enough hands in training to successfully manipulate a very severe bit. In the illustrations, Figures 47 and 48, the bosal is used with the spade bit which is a very severe bit. Trainers of the stock horse often use this type of bit. Professional trainers are more apt to use this bit as they are experienced. One must be extremely light handed to do so.

Now that your pleasure horse is well schooled in his gaits and bridled, you can teach him to neck rein. This should be the last phase of your horse's training, even if you are training a stock horse, as we shall see later.

Many trainers teach the horse to neck rein by crossing the reins under the horse's neck. If you want your horse to turn left, tighten the right rein across his neck and keep the left rein slack, with only a light pull. The horse will turn left because he has been trained to turn with pull on the left rein, however, he will come to associate moving away from the pressure on his neck as well. Pet him when he responds correctly. As he learns, he will associate turning with only the pressure on his neck, thus he has learned to neck rein.

You may then be able to carry the reins in your left hand only and your horse will turn in the direction you want him by merely laying the rein on his neck on the opposite side. Western pleasure riding then becomes simple, the horse turns with the rein on his neck and with your leaning, which is what Westerners call "rolling with the reins."

We will now turn to some of the basic principles of developing the stock horse, including the half turns, spin and sliding stop. Most trainers feel that the sliding stop is the most difficult and some authorities feel it is never taught as well without a bridle. They admit, however, that it may harden the mouth. As pointed out by one breeder of Quarter Horses, the principle of the sliding stop requires a bit. This horseman explains that to make a correct sliding stop, the horse's rump must come in low as the hind feet slide in well under the horse. The hackamore tends to hold his head and shoulders down, while they have to be up to get the rump down. Consequently, the principle of a flexed and higher head accelerates the rear portion of the body coming in lower as the horse stops. The horse trained in hackamore is taught all the stock horse arts and then goes into his bridle.

Trainers feel that it takes at least a year or more to train the horse to turn and spin on his hind feet and make a sliding stop. Therefore a horse may perform in hackamore at shows until he is five years old. The object of using the hackamore is to have him completely trained and then bridled. In this way he starts out in bridle with a completely fresh mouth.

In training your stock horse, begin with teaching him his gaits as we have described. Use only the hackamore and snaffle bit in training. In the earliest phase of training, teach the colt to respond to a hard pull on the rein and immediate release in regard to stopping and turning. Build up from this fundamental to turns on the hind feet with forefeet in mid-air and bringing him to a straight sliding stop.

Begin by training the colt to turn completely around when you are working him on the longe or in long-lines attached to either a snaffle or hackamore. He is taught to turn around in both directions, with a firm pull and immediate give in the rein. By small tugs, get him all the way around.

If he is taught this maneuver in the snaffle, to get him used to hackamore, trainers put hackamore and snaffle on and use them both, finally substituting the hackamore for the snaffle rein. Pressure to make the colt answer will be on his nose and chin bones.

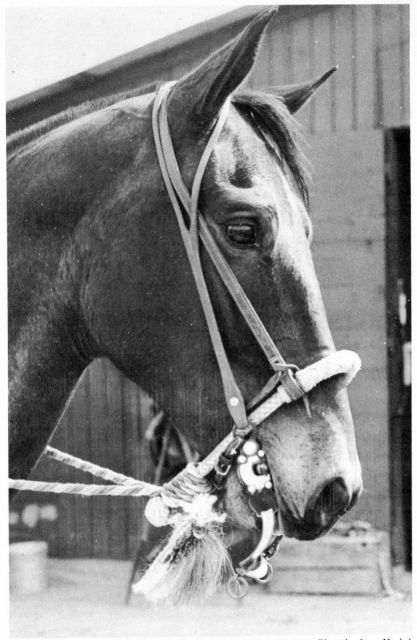

Photo by Ivan Mashek

FIG. 47   The bosal hackamore used in teaching the horse to use a curb bit. Notice the horse has on both bridle and bosal.

Photo by Ivan Mashek

Fig. 48   When the hackamore is off and you are using the curb bit, if training a stock horse still use a cavesson or bosal around the horse's nose to keep
him from opening his mouth in the bridle alone.

He will respond to pressure on these areas as he will to pressure on his mouth. These areas can also be hardened and made less sensitive, consequently you must use care in hard pulling just as you would with a bit. If these areas lose their sensitiveness, the horse will not readily respond.

To further teach him to respond by pull and release on the hackamore, tie a long rope on the lead line of his hackamore. Have him lope down a fence where you suddenly give him a hard pull with immediate release. The colt will not be able to stop and turn around immediately, but keep on with intermittent smaller tugs to stop him and get him turned around the way he came. When he is turned around, lope him down the fence in the opposite direction and do the same thing.

As the colt learns, he will begin to stop with the first pull and it need not be so hard. The same principle is used for quick stop when mounted. After he has progressed in his hackamore so that you can work him mounted, use the same principle. In teaching him to turn, pull one rein hard and slack the other, but not so much as to lose contact for he will turn his head. Your object is for him to turn but keep his head straight. Release the rein immediately when he answers you.

To aid in teaching him to turn on his hind feet, lope him slowly down beside a board fence or the barn. Give a firm pull and relax on the rein turning him into the barn. He will have to drop his head as he comes around. With the first pull on the rein, the colt begins to stop and his feet go under him slightly. As he learns, the distance required to stop will become shorter and shorter and it will finally require only one pull and relaxing of the rein to stop. Your object is to stop and turn him in almost one motion.

In teaching him to turn into the barn, as he stops to turn with the pull of the rein, make him wait momentarily for another pull in signaling him to turn. (See Figure 49.) Keep signaling him until he has turned around. You can then take him down the fence or barn in the opposite direction. Some trainers scare him to get him to jump out straight just before he has turned around. They do this to teach him to keep his body straight.

This maneuver of turning into the barn is repeated over and over and as the colt learns, he will associate the firm pull and relaxing the rein with stopping and turning. He learns to turn on his hind feet with his forefeet up. The barn being in front of him tends to make him turn more sharply. These movements will be slow at first. Do not work him every day in these lessons as they can easily be overdone. Twice a week is often enough.

After the colt learns to answer his signals, your job is to speed him up on his turns. Some trainers tap him on the shoulder with a small whip to make him turn faster. When he has turned around completely, then a tap on the rump starts him off quickly the way he came. As he learns to turn quickly, he will also begin to associate weight shift with turning.

It is the speed up in turning that makes him eventually able to turn half way around, and the jumping out that will help straighten him up. He learns to do the whole maneuver with the signal of a pull and release of the rein and with weight change. This is why a hackamore is used as it will not harden his mouth.

In training he learns to give himself the momentum or push to start his turns with his forefeet and as he turns on his hind feet, his forefeet are in mid-air. His hind feet remain in one spot.

To increase his ability to turn on his hind feet, trainers also gallop him in smaller and smaller circles. Finally the circle becomes so small that he can swing around on his hind feet. The pull and relax on the rein will still be his signals, however. Keep using these signals to go in smaller and smaller circles. Finally he will come to make the half-turn swinging around on his hind feet. All of this takes many, many months of painstaking training, with constant repetition. As time goes on he will slide further and further on his stop and be able to do a half turn from a standing position. For show, you will want to teach him to run down the rail coming to a straight sliding stop, then turn away from the rail and face the way he came. He must then run down the rail and do the same thing at the other end. Following this he will come up in front of the judge and make a quarter-turn to the right, a half-turn to the left and a half-turn to right.

After about a year of this training if your colt is able to respond to the signals of the rein to both stop and turn, you may finally introduce him to the bridle. This is done as we have explained earlier. However, before he is bridled you should begin to bring

Courtesy Bud Landrum, trainer
Photo by Ivan Mashek

Fig. 49　In training your horse to turn, school him at the side of the barn where he will have to turn sharply and drop his head as he comes around.

the reins in closer and to hold him in such a way that the rein is short and taut on the side toward which you are turning. The other rein is loose and comes up in position just about where the rein will fall when he learns to neck-rein. At this time, however, trainers do not bring pressure to bear on his neck as in teaching him to neck-rein. But, as time goes on, he will actually be performing on the neck-rein in picking up his forefeet and turning correctly. Shortening the reins will help to keep his head and neck straight in turning.

After he is bridled, you will need to continue working diligently on the sliding stop as it takes a long time to perfect. It is helpful to work on the stop in one fenced in corner of the training area. Never vary the spot where you ask him to stop and he will associate stopping with this spot. Some trainers have him shod only behind. His forefeet thus become tender and he will slide in better on his hind feet. You want him to actually slide without his forefeet bouncing along.

It is advisable to do special work on the sliding stop toward the end of his lesson period when he is beginning to tire. He will be more receptive to stopping. At the beginning take him into his stops from a lope. Pick up on the reins to stop him when his forefeet are off the ground before landing as this naturally makes his feet slide in some. If you wait until his forefeet are down, he must make another stride before he can stop. As you pick up on the reins, keep his head flexed, his chin tucked and hold them steady and taut to bring him into a straight sliding stop.

Perfect his sliding stop by repeating it over and over. As he learns gradually increase your speed until you can drive him into a gallop or run and make a straight sliding stop. The aid of the fence corner will help keep him straight when going down the fence and to stop him. Notice the trainer in Figure 50. In this illustration the sliding stop is in good form, however the horse's head is too high. His nose should be tucked and head flexed. It will take many months to get a young horse to make his stops in correct form.

The feats we have told you about are what is known as dry work. He is stopping and turning but is not actually working cattle. As these maneuvers require split-second timing, the spade

bit, which is very severe, is commonly used. You must be extremely light handed to consider using such a bit. You do not
want your horse to be afraid of his mouth or to be hurt with the
bit.

After your horse is finished in all the arts we have talked about
and has been taught to neck-rein, you may then teach him what
to do when you rope a sack.

To do this, tie a rope to the saddle horn and run it through a
rope tied around the horse's neck near the throatlatch. Taking
the end of the rope, you circle around the horse but keep him
facing you as you go around. You can have his bridle reins tied
loosely up on his neck at this time. If he steps toward you as you
go around, tap him on the chest with the rope, until he moves
back and takes up the slack in the rope. He must be taught to
keep the rope tight.

You may now mount and substitute a sandbag for yourself in
front of the horse. Then teach the horse to face the sandbag and
run past it with you mounted and jerk it down. Let the horse
drag the sandbag which will teach him to pull from the saddle.
You can then begin to throw the rope from the saddle, lassoing
your sandbag and bringing the horse to a sliding stop. Jump to
the ground as if to tie the calf. If the horse shows any tendency to
move forward, tap him with the rope. Some trainers use various
gimmicks to teach him to stay in place, such as a spring at his head
which sets off if he moves forward and hits him in the face, causing him to move backwards promptly.

In training your trail horse, you need not bother with turns
and spins, sliding stops and roping. Train your horse to pick his
way through mud, over ditches, strange objects, rocky trails, logs,
stand for opening gates and generally to proceed through rough
terrain without slipping or losing balance. He must be sure-
footed, obedient and trustworthy. Range horses have performed
this job especially well.

Western type horses do not wear long toes. They do wear a
little height on their heels and their shoes may be slightly longer
than the horse's heel, where they are ridden over rough ground.
This heel in back protects the foot. Most farriers shoe them with
ready made light weight shoes.

Courtesy Bud Landrum, trainer
Photo by Ivan Mashek

FIG. 50　The young horse is being schooled in making a straight sliding stop after he is allowed to wear a bridle. He has learned to bring his hind feet well in under him as he slides. However, he will need continued work in keeping his head flexed and chin tucked as he stops.

TRAINING THE PONY

Small ponies are often not as well finished as the horse, chiefly because of their size. They are too small for trainers to ride. However, there is growing interest in perfecting these miniature animals and expert trainers over the country are turning out remarkably fine products. In some big shows you will see them performing with brilliance and action.

The pony has great strength for his size and is unusually sound. A 40 inch pony can easily pull a cart with a man, whereas only a small child could go astride. Consequently, the Shetland's finished training is largely through hitching and driving. We pointed out that driving is unmatched as a device for training the Saddle Bred to go with balance and action and the same is true for the pony. Trainers have them going under harness like miniature Saddle Breds in fine harness.

The Shetland being a child's pet is generally ridden and driven by small children. For this reason, it is manners, rather than the high action required for other harness ponies that is emphasized at most shows. However, as they are being trained similarly to Saddle Bred horses and shod with various weighting devices to increase action, they are developing more finished gaits.

The Welsh pony runs a little larger than the Shetland and makes a fine little hunter and hack. Trainers of this breed say that he can be trained more like the horse as he moves more like one. His stride is longer and his trot is not the "pitty-pat" going of the Shetland. Welsh and Arab as well as Thoroughbred crosses also make good hunters for children.

The pony size of any breed of riding horse is trained just as you would train the horse. These may be pony sized Saddle Breds, Tennessee Walkers, Arabs, Thoroughbreds and so on. They are trained to be used by children in the same way adults use the horse.

The Shetland is far more prevalent in this country than other breeds of small ponies and we shall confine our remarks to methods of training the Shetland for riding and driving, and to the Welsh as trained for hunting and jumping.

In training the Shetland, you must study and know your pony

just as you would if training a horse. You know basically that your animal will be trustworthy, sure-footed and will learn readily. Most trainers say that he will learn faster than the horse. He will try from the start to do what you want and will be generally quiet as he is not a spirited and high strung animal.

Trainers put the halter on young Shetlands soon after they are born and handle them early. They become a pet and never have to be broken. Begin training by teaching him to lead on the halter and stand quietly. This can be done before he is weaned, but not much training should be undertaken before he is two because Shetlands are considered colts until three years old. It is unwise to saddle before two. Their bones are too soft to carry weight before that time.

English authorities claim that they don't reach maturity until eight or nine years of age and in that country they have not been allowed to be registered in the English Stud Book if over 42 inches at four years. In the United States the pony is registered in the American Shetland Club Stud Book at the time he is two. He is believed to have most of his height by that time. The quality of the Shetland has been improved considerably in this country and rules vary in the American and English Stud Books.

To train the Shetland, begin much as you do with a horse in getting him used to a snaffle bit. Let him wear it in the stall with a "bitting rig" or let him wear it with his halter. After he is used to the bit and will lead easily, you can then begin training him in long-lines. The bridle and lines probably will not be too novel for him if you will have someone lead him while you go behind. Work slowly with him and gradually begin teaching him to "get up" and "whoa." You will teach him to turn and be guided with the reins just as you have the horse. Keep your assistant working with you and leading him until he can answer all your commands and go in his gaits.

When you have driven him in long-lines until he understands your commands and can be guided, you can then get ready to hitch and drive him. Some of the better trainers wait until he is approaching three to have him pull a cart, as they believe he needs more strength. Since this is the way to develop balance and action, you want to drive and keep driving once you start.

Many trainers have very small children who are good riders and their children often work these ponies in their gaits under saddle. The pony does the walk, trot and canter and can be started under saddle at two.

If you are training your pony to be driven in the show ring, you will need to train him in what is called a park trot, which is a slow, showy trot with high action. Be careful in training not to trot at too great a speed. School him to respond with this gait and then be able to extend his trot and move on. Trainers say that he sacrifices his action if he is allowed to go with too much speed. The brilliance and action of the pony under harness is developed by constant repetition through driving. Driving will also help to finish his gaits under saddle, particularly his trot.

To help the pony go with action, he may be shod with "rocker" shoes. These shoes are heavy in the middle and taper off to almost nothing in front and behind. Blacksmiths will warn you not to let these shoes be put on unless heated, otherwise they won't fit. The quarter boot is also worn by the Shetland when being driven.

After the pony is going well in his gaits, you may put on a curb bit to keep his head up and in position. You will no doubt notice that the pony is trained similarly to the horse, using similar tack, only pony size.

The Welsh pony is often said to be almost too spirited for the average child. Mrs. Drury of Foxhollow Stables one of Virginia's foremost breeders of the Welsh, pooh-poohs this as a fallacy. She finds them very good and obedient with children. The one or two she has known in her experience to be "knot-heads," she attributed to the individual animal rather than the breed.

The smallest Welsh ponies may run 11.2 hands or 46 inches, but usually they run 52 to 54 inches. They are also trained like a horse and have the spirit to pick up their feet like a horse. Some trainers will put the halter on for a few minutes on the day of birth. The object is to never let the pony become afraid of a human being. Teach him to lead even as a suckling colt. We know trainers who will put a light child on them after they are yearlings and work them, but of course not strenuously. However, we suggest that you wait until two to saddle. You may work him in the corral or drive in long-lines, but do not mount.

At the time you do teach him to go under saddle, you may also teach him to jump small obstacles but not mounted. He may be taught with the aid of a circular chute inside of a small corral. In other words, when the pony is inside the chute, there is no way that he can go except forward and in a circle as the walls of the chute are on each side of him. The trainer lays small poles in his path in the chute and as he goes around, he must step over them. At first the trainer leads him around. When he will go quietly while being led, and has got the idea of stepping over the poles, let him go along without being led. Then go behind him with a switch and move him along. Increase his speed so that he will begin to hop over the poles. If he is sound, he is worked twenty minutes in the morning and twenty minutes in the afternoon.

The pony is trained in a walk, trot and canter. A collected canter may be hard for you. He must be trained to go straight with an extended stride. This is where a good child rider and trainer are necessary. When the pony is going well in his gaits, he must be taught to use a double bridle or a pelham as he is not allowed to be shown in hack classes without a curb. It is sometimes hard to get him collected, but when he gets the idea, he has no trouble.

Hunter training may be done as we have outlined for your horse. The pony is hacked through the woods and fields and under saddle is allowed to take small fences, no higher than the jumps in the school area. However, we would not start this before he is three and you have begun to jump him mounted. Ponies under 11.2 hands are not allowed to jump over two feet and those up to 13 hands, not over two and one-half feet. For their size, ponies are said to be able to jump higher than horses. You will work on the way he approaches his fences just as you would with your horse. Even the hunter hack is asked to take two fences as well as go in his gaits. You may also train and show your pony as a jumper. These little ponies sometimes have to jump off their ties and jumps may be raised slightly over the height we told you in arranging the jump offs.

For jumping, a little racing bridle with a dee bit or a big ring snaffle is adequate. It is best for children to use an English hunting saddle with safety stirrups. These stirrups unfasten should the child spill, and his foot cannot be caught in the stirrup. In training, it is useful to have an English felt saddle as the child rider can feel the pony's movements.

If you plan to alter your Welsh stallion, it is said to be better to wait until he is a yearling for it makes a better crust at the neck. Those altered earlier seem to have a lighter, thinner neck.

Your pony is apt to be better dispositioned if you let him out of the stall each day into a paddock or a pasture. He gets bored penned up in the stall. It's worth the extra grooming to have your pony happy. Unless you live in an area where the temperatures are severe, your pony can be out almost every day. The pony came from rugged country and propagated for centuries in cold weather.

CHAPTER X

Riding

In previous chapters we have tried to give you some understanding of the different breeds of horses you may ride and how they are cared for and trained. Now let's turn to a few of the fundamentals of riding the different seats with the understanding that this chapter cannot teach you to ride.

To learn to ride well, you must go to a competent instructor and patiently follow his guidance. Attend riding classes regularly. Spend some time around the stables. Take care of your own horse. All good horsemen must have knowledge of the care of horses and equipment and stable management.

Keep up your interest by going to horse shows. There you will observe skilled riders in action. A good rider cannot be made in a week. It is a long pull, but the exercise and enjoyment derived from learning will pay dividends.

The instructor at a good stable will always give a beginner a quiet, well trained horse which will respond readily to leg and rein signals. He probably will ride along with you at first to give you confidence.

In the beginning you will be taught to mount and dismount properly. To mount correctly, stand on the near side of your horse, about at his shoulder, facing to the rear. Hold your reins in your left hand across the horse's withers. Take hold of the left stirrup with the right hand and place your left foot in it. With your right hand on the cantle of the saddle, push up with your right foot and your left knee against the horse's shoulder. Now that you are straight up in the stirrup on your left foot, bend your right knee and throw your right leg over the horse's back and settle gently into the saddle.

Unless you have a physical defect, mount without a step or

fence. Very few people, except children, are unable to mount a 16 hand horse if they will but try.

To dismount, hold your reins in your left hand across your horse's withers. As you stand up in your left stirrup, take hold of the front of the saddle with your right hand and with your right knee bent, throw it over the saddle. Straighten it out as you do. Your body will be leaning slightly over the saddle. Then grasp the back of the saddle with your right hand, take your left foot out of the stirrup and let yourself slowly down.

When you have gained confidence and begin to feel at home on a horse's back, the importance of the hands and seat will be stressed.

The seat, including the position of your legs, the pressure areas against the saddle, and adjustment of stirrup leathers can be learned through instruction and practice only. It is in the seat that you learn to balance yourself. Later on, with firm knee pressure, you will find that you can ride even without stirrups.

Your reins should never be used to "hold on to." You get security wholly through the seat when you are sitting balanced in the saddle. Your position is such that your weight is distributed from your seat to your stirrups with your thighs firmly against the saddle and rolled inward slightly so that you can take firm hold with your knees. You must first of all gain balance in the saddle before you are free enough to work much with reins and the horse's mouth.

As we have mentioned earlier, there are different seats for riding. A rider sits these seats because they have been found to facilitate the job the horse is to do and are generally more comfortable for the rider. These various seats are: saddle horse or park seat, hunting seat, forward seat and stock saddle seat. As a beginner you will not be concerned with the forward seat and jumping.

The park seat is used to ride three- and five-gaited horses as well as any breed where the English flat saddle is used. Sitting this seat, you should be erect and in the center of your saddle. Your shoulders, hips and ankles should fall in about a straight line over each other. The stirrups should be adjusted so that when your legs are well extended and are then brought up to the stirrups there is only a slight bend of the knee. Your stirrups will be fairly long with weight pressure flat on the ball of your foot. The stirrups help to give you balance in this position.

Your upper legs or thighs lie firmly against the saddle and are slightly rolled inward so that your knees are brought into position for firm pressure against the saddle. Your heels should be slightly down and your toes turned slightly out.

The hunting seat is not too different except that it is more forward. The saddle is built so that the seat is inclined forward. Your back should be straight but your body should lean slightly forward causing the rear of the buttocks to be raised off the saddle. To balance you in this position, the stirrups are shorter, striking you about ankle length. Thus you have a greater bend of the knee to grip securely in the saddle and the line of your body is still in a balanced position over your stirrups. The ball of your foot may be well into the stirrup irons, or the irons may touch your heel. This latter is what is known as the foot being "fully home." The bottom of your foot may also be turned slightly outward. Your thighs are rolled inward and your knees exert firm pressure. In this position your weight can be more on the horse's shoulder when jumping, where he can carry it with least effort. In jumping your body should be inclined forward in line with your horse's body as he negotiates the obstacle.

The forward seat is an extreme of the hunting seat used for jumping. Your stirrups are much shorter and your seat well forward. Your knees are also well forward and braced against the knee roll. As you jump you are up over the horse's neck with your weight on his shoulders and completely off his back and quarters as he jumps. In this position your weight is such that the horse is able to get off the ground with greater ease and to fold up with less likelihood of touching the obstacle.

The stock saddle seat is different but more like the park seat. The Western saddle being deep with high pommel and cantle permits little movement. You are literally "in a chair." You should sit erect with your shoulders over your hips in a straight line. You should appear relaxed and comfortable. Your stirrups are quite long so that your legs are almost straight, but slightly forward to

Fig. 51   The Saddle Horse seat or Park seat as illustrated by Olwen Beach, first winner West of the Mississippi River, of Reserve Championship in a Medal Class (Saddle Seat equitation) for 17-year-olds or under at Madison Square Garden, New York City.

Fig. 52   The hunting seat, using forward seat saddle. Notice the short stirrups, knees well bent and soles of boots turned slightly out, and heels down.

the stirrups. In this position your heels are only slightly down. The horn of the saddle was devised for roping cattle and its presence is of no value in riding for pleasure.

After you begin to get some balance and security of seat, your instructor will doubtless begin to work on your hands and their part in guiding, controlling and keeping your horse collected. When you feel firm and secure in your seat, you can give more attention to the reins. To have "light hands" or "good hands" you must first have a good secure seat.

The Saddle Horse is commonly ridden with the double bridle. Therefore you hold a rein to the curb bit and a rein to the snaffle in each hand. The snaffle is used to control and guide but give your horse greater freedom. The curb is to control, get flexion of the head as well as steady him in his gaits.

If you are riding a Tennessee Walker or a Western type horse, you will doubtless use only a curb bit and the one set of reins. You may also use only one set of reins attached to the snaffle in riding a hunter or jumper.

One of the first things you must learn is that the bits, especially the curb, can hurt your horse's mouth. It rests on the tender bars and when the curb rein is pulled, the cheek piece or shank is like a lever that causes the bit to press down on the bars and the curb chain to exert pressure under the chin. Hard pulling can thus be painful. You must use reins with sympathy. In riding with short reins they should be firm but not tight, with just enough contact to keep the animal responsive. You will notice that tightening the curb will instantly make your horse hold his head up, flex and tuck his chin. This head position is that of collection and in the show ring your horse should always carry his head in this position. If you pull too hard, however, he is likely to pull his chin too far in, throw his mouth open and generally makes an ugly spectacle. When he responds to your pressure with the rein, release it as he has answered you.

To keep him alert, you will have to tighten the reins intermittently and also use your legs. Intermittent taps with the heel will help to keep him "up in the bit" and walking in an alert manner.

When using a double bridle, both sets of reins will come into your hands, but how you hold them is at your discretion, as they may be separated by different fingers. The reins are separated so that you can get the desired action on each bit.

Your instructor will need to show you how to hold them. The fingers you use to separate them may be those least awkward for you. Many people like to have the snaffle come into their hands on the outside or under the little finger, with the curb running over all the fingers secured between the first finger and thumb. The reins can be tightened by bending the wrists. Keep your wrists flexible and your hands in such a position that your thumbs are upward. How high your carry your hands will depend on where the horse carries his head. Generally your hands are carried a few inches above the saddle.

To shorten your reins, take hold of the reins you want to shorten with your thumb and forefinger of the opposite hand, so your hand is free to take them up the desired distance. Do the same thing with the opposite hand. To lengthen them, let them slide through your hand.

If you are riding with only one set of reins, they may come into your hands either on the outside of your little finger, or between the third and little finger. If you are riding Western saddle with only one set of reins, show rules require your left hand to be "around the reins." Your left arm should be carried naturally and bent at the elbow so that your hand will be just above the pommel of the saddle. You will ride with a reasonably loose rein, meaning longer reins. Your right arm may rest comfortably on your thigh.

As we have mentioned earlier, you move your horse into his gaits by use of "aids." They are your signals that tell him what to do. Therefore, the "aids" are your reins or hands, legs, voice and weight. We have seen in training the horse that the trainer starts out with simple voice commands and as training progresses, the horse learns to respond to the reins, legs and weight as well as voice. A good horseman becomes so skilled in applying the "aids" that observers can barely tell they are being used. This is the perfected art that you strive for.

Before using "aids" or signaling your horse to do something,

FIG. 53   Stock saddle seat exhibited by Luann Beach, winner of Reserve
Championship Medal Class, West Coast.

"collect" or "gather" him. This will make him alert and he will be waiting for your signal to tell him what to do. To "gather" him, tighten the reins slightly so that he feels the bit and at the same time squeeze your legs to his sides. Do not keep a steady pressure with the reins and legs but make it recurrent until your horse responds. Then signal him to move.

To move out into a walk, slacken the reins slightly, squeeze your legs giving him a nudge with your heels. You may also lean slightly forward in your seat. To stop use almost the opposite signals. First gather your horse, then brace your back toward the rear of the saddle, tighten your reins by bending your wrists toward you and at the same time lightly squeeze your legs to his sides. You will learn in riding that pressure on the bit is always accompanied by some leg pressure.

To go into the trot use the same aids that you did to walk except increase the firmness of pressure with the calves of your legs or give a firm kick with your heels. Most horses also are trained to trot on voice commands. As you become used to your horse, you may not have to use all these signals for him to respond, but keep using whatever signals you do apply until he trots out as you want him to.

Unless you are riding Western saddle, it is always correct to post the trot. Your posting should be in rhythm with the movements of your horse. Balance and good riding come from following the movements of your horse. At the trot you will begin to learn the real meaning of this.

As we have explained, the horse trots on diagonal pairs of legs. That is, his right fore leg and left hind leg rise and descend simultaneously as does his left fore leg and right hind leg. This causes an up and down motion which will jar and bounce you in the saddle. To eliminate this bouncing, both for your comfort and that of the horse, you rise and descend from the saddle as he makes his strides. That is, you rise with one beat and descend with the second beat. You do not land heavily in the saddle as you descend but only lightly meet it. Thus, by posting you have no jarring sensation but a smooth ride. The jar is absorbed by your knees and ankles. Keep your knees and thighs firmly pressed against the saddle, straightening your knees slightly as you rise with pressure in your stirrups. Your rise is facilitated by the horse gently throwing you up as he goes.

Doubtless, you will be awkward at first and will rise too far out of the saddle. As you learn, you will get the feel of the horse's movement and can post in rhythm with him. It will come to be scarcely discernible.

When you have learned to post well enough so that you have a secure seat and are in rhythm with your horse, you can turn attention to your reins and hands. Keep your reins taut enough to contact or feel the horse's mouth. If you are riding a Saddle Bred show horse, you will want to keep him trotting in a collected manner. Your reins should be short, his head flexed and he should go with action and form. He will be comfortable to ride and beautiful to watch but will not cover ground. To cover ground he will go at a longer, striding trot where he loses action. This is what happens when he is trotting too fast. To keep him at the right speed and head carriage, you will have to intermittently use your legs and reins. This art you will learn more about as you advance.

Another fundamental in riding at the trot is ability to recognize the diagonal pair of legs you are posting with, and to change from one to the other. In posting, you actually begin to rise in your stirrups just as the fore foot of the diagonal you are posting with touches the ground. Thus, you are rising up as your horse is making his stride forward and are down when these legs are down. This frees the horse of your weight as he strides out. To change. diagonals, sit momentarily, and pick up the opposite stride. Posting equally as much with one diagonal as the other will help keep your horse balanced.

If you are riding in a ring, make a practice of posting the diagonal next to the rail and you will post equally with both. Authorities on horsemanship maintain that if you post with this rail diagonal, it will help prevent a break in gait. In equitation classes you will be asked to figure eight at the trot and demonstrate change of diagonals. However if you are riding for pleasure, don't let this concern you too much for you will doubtless post with both diagonals anyway.

Though equestrians have slightly different aids for putting a horse into a canter, it is always correct to do as we told you in our chapter on Training. First gather your horse so that he will have his head up and his hocks under him, ready to respond. If you want him to take a left lead, turn his head slightly to the rail, touching him behind the girth with your right foot. Lean slightly forward to the left. This maneuver throws him enough off balance to make him naturally reach out with his left foreleg. He will do the same thing without the rail.

Some riders use only a tap in the elbow or a shift in weight. But whatever signals you use, use them continuously so your horse will know what you want.

The canter should be slow and rolling and you should sit close to your saddle following the movement of your horse. Keep him collected and control his speed. He will slightly roll forward as he goes because of the position of his legs at this three beat gait. You will have to keep your elbows flexible and let your hands move forward slightly with his head.

When you are going well at the canter and you want to push on into a gallop, raise up in your stirrups and lean well forward over his shoulders. A kick with the heel will increase his pace and drive him on.

If you are riding stock saddle seat, the lope is usually signaled by giving with the rein slightly and shifting your weight. As the Western type horse is a reining-horse, he is signaled into his movements by rein and weight. He goes on loose rein and the Western rider leans slightly in turning, in going forward, or stopping. He uses his legs to increase speed and keep the horse's haunches straight as do other equestrians.

After mastering the basic principles of riding, start riding different horses. This will give you confidence and permit you to test the use of aids you have learned. Endeavor to ride horses that are of proper size for your height and weight.

Children especially should be given careful instruction for habits formed at early ages linger on. Youngsters should not be hurried or forced to jump before they are ready. Confidence may be built up by permitting the child to advance as rapidly as he learns. Later on stirrup leathers may be removed to help in gaining a better seat and in teaching to grip with the knees.

If your instructor permits you to go out on trails, do not run the legs off the horse. Space your gaits, walk a while, trot and then walk and canter. Walk your mount for at least 10 minutes after leaving the stable and for a like time just prior to returning. This will help cool him out.

After you have progressed enough so that you can begin to learn the art of riding the gaited horse, the stock horse or begin jumping obstacles, there will be many new skills to perfect.

CHAPTER XI

Horse Shows

As an amateur planning to participate in a horse show for the first time, you may find some of the following hints helpful. When you receive notice a show is contemplated, write or call the secretary and ask for a premium list. This will indicate all the classes to be held, describe the conditions for showing in each class, the entry fees and prizes to be given.

Then go over the lists carefully. Check the classes you want to enter and fill out your entry blank. Consider only those for which your horse can qualify. Do not try to participate in more than six. It would be too hard on the horse. In smaller shows of only one day, you might show in no more than two classes. The chances are, if you are a beginner, that you won't be ready for large shows.

The classes you choose will depend largely on the type horse you are showing, his age, whether he has won ribbons before, his height, sex, his training and so on. Consider only those in which you have the best chance to make a good showing, and in which you will not be too far outclassed. (In large shows exhibitors often choose those that pay the largest prizes.)

If you are interested in competing in equitation classes in which your horsemanship is judged, rather than your mount, the premium list will indicate whether the classes offered are for saddle horse seat, stock saddle seat or hunting seat. The premium list will also give you a description and illustration of the jump courses over which you will be asked to show in the various classes. Some of the smaller shows do not always do this but will have the course mimeographed and give you a copy to study before the show.

Rules for showing and judging are generally those of the American Horse Shows Association. The American Horse Shows Association supplies its individual members and member shows with its rule book. A close study of its contents will prove very useful.

If you are showing a Saddle Bred, the classes you select will depend on whether your horse is three- or five-gaited, a road hack, a bridle path hack, a pleasure horse, or whether you will drive him in fine harness or in combination classes.

As a gaited horse, he must be able to do each of his three or five gaits separately and distinctly. If not, he is a pleasure horse. Remember, your gaited horse may be shown either as three-gaited or five-gaited but never as both. He is marked to help prevent this violation of show procedure. As mentioned before, the mane and upper part of the tail of the three-gaited or walk-trot horse is roached (clipped). The five-gaited retains his full mane and tail.

In fine harness classes you may show only the five-gaited type, with flowing mane and tail. Manners are his chief requisite, and he will be required to do only two gaits in the ring, the animated walk and park trot.

However, there may be combination classes offered in which you may drive your horse to an appropriate four-wheeled buggy, then unhitch in the ring and show him in his gaits under saddle. There are combination classes for both three-gaited and five-gaited and emphasis is on the trot when driven.

If you are showing your gaited horse under saddle, there will probably be many different classes in the premium list for which you may or may not qualify. Classifications may include junior classes in which your horse must not be over four years old, or perhaps three years old if three-gaited, classes for amateurs-to-ride, which eliminate professional competition, and classes for ladies in which the horse's suitability for a lady is considered, with emphasis on manners. If there are many Saddle Breds shown in your community, three-gaited classes may be broken down according to height such as, not exceeding 15 hands, over 15 hands but not exceeding 15.2 and over 15.2 This creates smaller classes wherein you have a better chance to win. Five-gaited classes are broken down according to sex and there may be classes for mares, geldings and stallions.

The show may offer other classes entitled maiden, novice, and

limit. Maiden classes require that you have not previously won a
blue ribbon in that division in shows recognized by AHSA; novice,
that you have not won more than two blue ribbons; and limit,
that you have not won more than five. Most shows will offer open
classes for both three- and five-gaited horses where you will have
no restrictions as to age, sex, amateurs, ladies or previous winnings.

One of the finest competitions in which to show your Saddle
Bred is the model class. Your horse is shown in hand and is judged
on conformation and finish only. Consequently, if yours has obvious faults of conformation, you would not want to compete in
this class.

The best of the show may be run off in the "stakes" at the end
of the show. This will be true for any breed or type, but there may
be stake classes for both three-gaited and five-gaited Saddle Bred
performers. The different stake classes determine the championship winners. These classes may be broken down by height and
sex in the case of gaited horses. Some shows will require that the
first two winners in each of the previous classes enter the stake or
forfeit their winnings.

If you are showing your Saddle Bred as a bridle path hack or as
a road hack, his classes and performance will be different from
those we have described. Your bridle path hack will be judged on
his ability to give you a pleasant ride. You will want to consider
his manners, how well he goes on a reasonably loose rein, at a collected trot, whether he will stand quietly and back readily.

In showing a road hack, you will let him go on loose rein with
extended stride and he will have to demonstrate real ability to
push on. Hunters are sometimes shown in this class in competition
with you. Your mount will be judged on substance and strength
as well as manners and performance. In other words, the horse's
ability to move on across country as a good road mount is considered.

If your saddle horse cannot be shown in any of the classes we
have mentioned, you may decide to show him in pleasure classes
where it matters not what he looks like. Now his manners and
obedience are paramount. Perhaps this is a good way to start as a
novice. For you can begin to develop some show presence and the

technique of showing before you advance to a horse of more perfection. Your pleasure horse need not be high grade Saddle Bred but may be of mixed origin. But he must be what the name implies, a pleasure to ride, responsive and under control.

We told you earlier that many Morgan horses are competing with Saddle Breds and doing well for themselves. Morgans, however, have their own classes and the same is true of the Arabs. If you have a Morgan, you may show him under saddle or you may drive him in fine harness. His performance will be emphasized more than quality and manners in most classes. You may choose to show him in classes designated by sex, or in height, or in novice, combination, fine harness, pleasure, "stake," stock horse or what is known as the versatile Morgan classes. In the latter, he is shown hitched and under saddle and must also jump two obstacles.

If you are entering an Arab, you may show him either in classes under English saddle or under Western saddle. Under English saddle the classifications will be similar to those already described for the Saddle Bred. The Arab is often shown in pair classes, in combination classes, as pleasure horse English type and Western type and as a park horse. In this latter class, their style, finish, quality, performance, manners and brilliance as Arabs are considered. You should have a really fine looking mount to enter this class. The Arab may also be shown in harness, in which case he is shown at a road gait in addition to walk and park trot.

Classes for the Tennessee Walking Horse are similar to those for gaited horses. There may be open classes, "stake," novice, amateur-to-ride, stallion, gelding, mare and junior classes. Performance is emphasized in Walking Horse competitions today. The Breeders' Association and now the AHSA have ruled that these horses are to be judged 40% on running walk, 20% on flat-footed walk, 20% on canter and 20% on conformation. This means that unless you are in a very small show in which the competition may not be keen, your horse must have good overstride and speed at the running walk to win. A twelve inch overstride a few years ago was considered average. However, with training methods today, unless his overstride is 36 inches, you may have such competition you would be better off in pleasure classes.

If you are choosing classes for a hunter, there are groupings

other than those we have described. You may want to show him
either as a conformation hunter or as a working hunter. In the
first, his conformation may count 40% toward his winnings and
any blemishes, scars or cuts will count against him. In the second,
his conformation does not count, but whether he maintains an
even hunting pace, his manners, way of going, style in jumping
and hunting soundness do. If he has these qualities it matters not
whether he has been scratched or has faults of conformation.

In considering a hunter's conformation, a judge will note his
strength and endurance as evidenced by depth and width of chest
area and will look to see if he has good pasterns. If too straight
they jar the rider; if too sloped, they will not stand up under tough
going. A hunter must be comfortable to ride. His ribs must not
be sprung out too far and his shoulders should be sloped, for a
straight shoulder gives an uncomfortable ride.

A short neck is also considered bad conformation. Hindquarters should be strong and well muscled, with muscled gaskins
which make him stronger and gallop faster. His legs should be
straight, joints flat and not too bony, with no curbs or calf hocks.
As we have told you before, no horse has perfect conformation.
You can judge your horse's shortcomings in conformation and
enter him in relation to the competition that you expect to meet.

Your choice of hunter classes may also depend on weight classifications—lightweight, middleweight, or heavyweight. You may
also have such classifications as green, regular and qualified. To
be green, the AHSA rules that he must not have been shown before January 1 of the year in which you are competing. In green
competition, fences will not exceed $3\frac{1}{2}$ feet. To qualify as a regular hunter your horse should be able to work over a hunt course
where he may be asked to jump up to $4\frac{1}{2}$ feet. As a qualified
hunter, he must have been regularly hunted for more than one
season with a pack of hounds.

Some of the classes you choose from may include schooling
classes open to all horses, with jumps not over $3\frac{1}{2}$ feet. Others
may be for Thoroughbreds, and other than Thoroughbreds, of
the different weight carrying classifications and different age
groupings. Or they may be designated as amateurs-to-ride,
maiden, novice, model, ladies hunters, open and Corinthian

classes. Unless you live in hunting country, you will probably not have the latter in your show, as you must be a member of a recognized Hunt, and appear in the proper attire of your hunt to qualify.

Most shows offer touch-and-out classes with perhaps eight fences at four feet, to be raised in case of tie.

Other than showing your hunter in classes over fences, you may also show him in his gaits. Such classes are as hunter hack, hunter under saddle, and bridle path hack. These classes are what their names signify—the hunter's ability to go in his gaits under saddle.

As a hunter hack, he is required to take two jumps in addition to being shown in his gaits. As a bridle path hack be sure he will stop easily, stand rock still while you mount and dismount, and back readily. The judge may call for this performance.

Classifications for jumpers are not so involved as for hunters. They generally include open, lady, amateur, knock-down-and-out, handy, scurry and "stake" classes. Handy and scurry classes require you to jump against time. In knock-down-and-out classes you win if your horse clears the most obstacles without a knock down. A refusal or run-out is counted as a knock down.

If you are choosing classes in which to show a Western pleasure horse or a stock horse, you will notice there are still classes other than these we have talked about. Generally stock horse classes provide for the exhibitor to work under the direction of the judge. Some of the classes offered to stock horse exhibitors are hackamore, ladies and juniors. Classes are also divided according to the weight of your horse.

If you are showing a pony, your selection of classes will depend on the pony's size, whether you are showing him as a hunter, jumper, hunter hack, or as a saddle pony or under harness. Children's mounts are judged on the same basis as horses, except the small ponies for young children are judged primarily on manners and suitability for a child. Also the jumps for children are lower, their height depending on the size classification of the pony. A child should be able to enter such classes as musical chairs, races, boy and girl teams, family teams, bare back and fancy turnout. The premium list will carefully describe the conditions.

After you have carefully checked the classes for which your mount is qualified, and in which you want to enter, enclose a check for the entry fee and return your entry blank. The fees are usually quite reasonable.

If you are showing in a small community or club show in your vicinity, you may be able to take your horse over for afternoon or evening classes and return him to his stable. It may be even close enough for you to ride over to the grounds, but if not you will have to use a horse trailer. If it is a large show of several days duration away from your community, you may be notified by the show secretary where to stable your horse at the show grounds, where you can purchase feed and other pertinent data.

If the show is quite a distance from your home, it is better if you plan to arrive at the show grounds at least a day before the show is to begin. By arriving early, your horse will have a chance to get a good rest before the show. This is especially important if you have to travel far. You will also have an opportunity to accustom him to the ring in which he is to be shown.

If your horse is to be taken even one hundred miles, it is best to bandage his legs before starting out with him. Some horsemen recommend Tuttle's elixir and alcohol as a "brace" or leg wash. Apply this preparation to the legs using sheet cotton and bandage wrapped around the legs tight enough to prevent slipping down. The bandage will protect his legs in the trailer and keep them in good condition for the show. It is also advisable to cover the floor of your trailer with sand. If you are transporting your horse to a show and returning the same day, have him well groomed and ready before leaving home. If you will be away overnight you may have the mane of your hunter braided, ready to pull and tie the ribbons after you arrive. Cover him with a blanket in transit, to keep his coat lying flat.

If you are to be away from your home stable a few days, take your special tonics or feeds with you as these items are often unavailable on short notice. There is usually a farrier and veterinarian at all shows, but it is best to attend to any shoeing or other matters pertaining to the animal before leaving your home stable.

After getting settled at the show grounds, go to the horse show office. In a small show this might be either a tent or a stall in the barn. Check with the office on your events, noting any time change or change in schedule. At this time you might receive the "number" that you are to wear in the show ring, or be told when you will get it. Each horse you enter in the show is assigned a number. You can also get other show information there.

Remember, the purpose of a horse show is to show your horse, so have him looking his best, and be equally as well turned out yourself. You want him to have that extra bloom that will make him show to his best advantage. For a month or two months (depending on his condition) before you plan to show him, gradually increase his grain ration if he has been on pasture and work him in his gaits. Jump him or practice any arts that he has been schooled in. Work him at least an hour a day. If he is a young, green hunter or jumper you may want to school him over his jumps two or three times a week. For an older horse that knows his job, once a week may be sufficient. Work in long-lines or on the longe is good exercise at this time. Polish him up on changing his gaits, leads at the canter, answering your signals, backing, his running walk or any other arts in which he may be required to show proficiency.

Most owners will time their preparation period to end the last day or two days before the show. The exercise periods on these days may be no longer than 15 minutes. During this preparation period some stables bandage the horse's legs at night and use leg "braces" or medications to keep legs sound.

Also during this conditioning period, groom him daily and blanket him in the evenings to put his coat in top shape. Two or three days before the show you may have a professional clip him. In other words, you want no long hairs about his head, ears, legs or feet and want a sleek, silky coat.

Your horse may carry his stable colors if you desire. Five-gaited and Tennessee Walkers show their colors by plaiting the forelock and upper lock of the mane with a ribbon representing their stable. To plait the lock of mane, take three ribbons and plait with it, tying the ribbon slightly before reaching the end. The ribbons from the mane and forelock should fall well down on the neck. This plaiting is done only for the show ring. Brush his mane and tail well to have them long and flowing. You may use a colored browband. The three-gaited wears no ribbon as his mane is roached, but he may wear a colored browband.

The hunter and jumper are prepared for show by braiding the entire mane in small braids down the neck, and braiding his tail. You will try to have seven braids, eight with the forelock on the mare and twelve on a gelding. Braid the tail to the end of the dock and cut or pull it to about a man's two fists below the horse's hocks. You may use colored yarn to tie the braids if you wish. However, he will appear quite handsome if the yarn you tie the braid with is dark and doesn't show. To braid the mane, take a lock, dampen it and plait almost to the end. Then place in it two strands of ribbon which have been knotted together at one end. Loop the ribbon around the braid to fasten it. Then double the lower part of the braid under and tie with the end of the ribbon. Have all the loops of braids the same length.

Ponies are dressed like the saddle horse, the hunter, or whatever division he is showing in. Your Western horse should wear no ribbons or braids.

Your own dress for the show will depend upon the mount you are showing and whether he is competing in Saddle Bred classes, hunting and jumping events, Western classes or fancy turnout. It is an old adage that the "horse doesn't care what you wear," but you should be plainly and correctly dressed. In Saddle Bred classes, it is correct to wear hat, tie and gloves in all events. This includes men, women and children. In many small shows where not so much emphasis is placed on dress, especially in pleasure classes, women and children often wear plain sport shirts with no hat or gloves.

To go ahead with what is considered correct, however, for daytime wear in gaited classes, fine harness, under saddle or model and in horsemanship events, the jodhpur breeches, Kentucky or peg top cut, with matching or contrasting riding coat is worn. Jodhpur breeches should be accompanied by black or tan jodhpur boots with elastic sides or straps. These boots come just about the ankle. Most followers of the Saddle Bred shows prefer the tight fitting Kentucky type jodhpur breeches with matching coat. The Kentucky jods do not have the peg top and in place of a cuff are bell shaped at the bottom.

To complete the daytime outfit, a felt hat, white shirt with a plain or horse figured tie, and gloves suitable to the weather, are proper. It is permissible for ladies driving in either day or night events to wear street attire.

A short riding whip, about thirty-six inches, is carried while riding in five-gaited classes and the niegheri or rattan stick is carried in three-gaited events. The riding crop is not carried in gaited events but may be carried for jumping.

The daytime riding clothes may also be used for night events. However, some exhibitors, both men and women, wear the tuxedo jodhpur riding suit with black bow tie. In these instances the derby is prescribed for five-gaited events while the high silk hat is worn for the three-gaited. This attire is generally not worn except in large shows. A boutonniere is permissible at all times.

In hunting events, a hunting cap may be worn in any event except appointment classes, or the hard top derby may be used. Medium buff riding breeches, tight fitting at the knee, are worn with hunting boots, which give support in jumping. Boot garters are always worn with hunting boots. A split-tailed black or oxford grey riding coat with plain or checkered vest, a four-in-hand tie or a stock, and gloves complete the outfit. Gloves may be brown string, pigskin or yellow. In Corinthian classes formal hunt attire is worn, and colors of the Hunt may be worn on the collar of a black hunting coat.

In Western classes, Western clothes are proper. These include Western trousers, called levis and Frontier pants. They are cut with fairly close fitting legs but are not so tight fitting as jodhpurs or riding breeches. They do not need to be tight as the rider does not post the trot. Elaborate Western shirts, or those of a more plain variety are worn, plus a vest if desired, Western hat, and in stock horse classes, chaps and Western boots. A coiled lariat is attached to the saddle.

There are certain manners, courtesies and customs to follow about the show ring, regardless of the size of the show. Remember, sportsmen are ladies and gentlemen. You are on common ground with other horse lovers, so introduce yourself to those persons you do not know. If the show is on your home ground, you are duty bound to make the visitors feel at home. You will expect the same treatment at their show. You will doubtless be invited to dinners, barbecues and other get togethers. Attend them but do not wear out your welcome. For the "horsey gentry" in the vicinity, it is the chance to play host that they have looked forward to and they will want to make your stay pleasant.

It is not good taste for you to ask every owner how much he paid for his horse. But it is permissible to ask the sale price of an animal if you are genuinely interested in buying.

Also do not make uncomplimentary remarks about another person's horse. It is not uncommon for an owner to place his love for his horse, or dog, far above monetary value, even though the animal may not look like much to you. In this vein we need only mention the poor taste of making disparaging remarks about other breeds that you do not happen to be interested in. This is so common among followers of the different breeds that we could not refrain from this advice.

There will be an amplifier attached to the barn or stable area and the announcer will notify you when to get ready for your class. Be sure your horse is saddled or hitched before your class is called and while waiting, you can warm him up. If you are showing a Tennessee Walker, you will enter the ring at a running walk and maintain it until the judge orders you to change. As it is necessary to warm your horse up from a walk before going into this gait, you should be careful to have him ready to enter the ring at his best. If you are showing a hunter or jumper, you will also want to exercise him outside the ring and get him ready and alert.

When your class is summoned, ride up to the "enter" gate at the ring. The gatemaster or ringmaster will have your class ready to enter the ring at the signal from the judge. Double check your person and tack. When the signal is given to enter the ring, if you are showing a Saddle Bred or Saddle Horse type, enter the ring at a brisk trot. It looks good to come in fast. It is also best to go into the ring at a trot with your hunter hack (though it should not be so brisk) because at a slower gait you may not have enough time to get the feel of the ring before the judge orders you to do something. An exception to this procedure is the Western horse, which comes in at a walk.

After entering the ring, go around to the right and stay close to the rail. Keep at a brisk trot with your Saddle Bred and if you find your horse overtaking another, pass him by riding to the left. If you find yourself getting bunched up, in order to avoid an accident, pull your horse out and cut across the center of the ring to the opposite side. This is perfectly permissible but do not ride down the judge or ringmaster in the maneuver.

After all of the contestants have entered the ring, the ringmaster will take over, giving commands as the judge directs him. When the change of gaits is ordered, do so promptly but not so quickly as to upset or confuse your mount. If your horse should break his gait, immediately start him over in the called for gait. This can happen to anyone, so do not let it disturb you.

When you are in the ring, give your horse or pony all of your attention. Ride with both hands unless you are riding Western saddle. In that case, hold the reins in your left hand. Do not talk or wave to anyone outside the ring. Be intent on getting the best performance out of your horse especially when you are in the judge's view. You will want speed at the rack and trot, especially with your five-gaited horse, but a smooth slow canter.

When you are showing in classes in competition with professional riders, you may find they have many tricks that they use in the ring that amateurs take a long time in learning. The amateur is usually taken up completely with riding and getting the most out of his mount, while a professional will always have one eye on the judge and oftentimes, his other eye on the horse he wants to beat.

If the professional does not happen to be riding a horse that will rack or trot as fast as the other contestants he would like to beat, he is apt to cut across the ends of the ring if the judge is not looking. If this same horse's canter is a bit fast, however, he may keep him right on the rail to make him appear slower. By doing this, it will take him longer to go around the ring and by cutting corners at the rack and trot, he will come around the ring faster. Thereby, he makes his mount look much better to the inexperienced observer.

Then, too, there is the riding down and trying to break the gaits of the other horse while passing. These are all old tricks and you should not be caught unawares when riding in the ring with professionals. We don't mean to infer that all professionals use these tricks. The ones that do are definitely in the minority. They are all good riders and rarely register complaints about each other. It is very interesting to watch them ride in shows and see how they jockey for position to cut a competitor out of the judge's view or get away from another rider who is endeavoring to ride them down. This is a business with these men and women and very often they are riding a horse that they have put a lot of effort and money into for several months or even years.

In smaller community and club shows where you will begin showing as a novice, you may not have this fast competition, but no doubt as you go along you will develop skill in showing that will tend to bring out the best in your horse in front of the judge. Be careful not to bunch up so the judge's view of you is obstructed. If your horse is not one that can go at peak performance all around the ring, try to keep an eye on the judge and when you are in his view, have your horse at his best.

After the judge has observed the gaits or special work, the contestants will be called to the center of the ring. In showing the Saddle Bred or Tennessee Walker, "park" or "stretch" your horse. Stay at least five feet from your neighbor. You were judged on performance, manners, way of going, quality, conformation or whatever the class stipulated. The awarding of the prizes and ribbons will follow immediately. Colors indicate winning sequence. A blue is first place, red second place, yellow third place and white fourth place.

If you are lucky enough to win a ribbon, take it when offered, thank the judge, and if a lady guest is honored by being permitted to give out the awards, tip your hat if you can do so safely. Saddle Bred riders, having both hands full of reins, usually place the ribbon between their teeth. After receiving the award, start for the rail at a fast trot. Go once around the ring and ride out. If there is a cash prize in addition to the ribbon, you may call for it later at the horse show office.

Essentially the same procedure will be followed in the ring if you are driving in fine harness classes.

Bring your Western type horse in at a walk. You will be asked to put him into a jog trot and lope, and perhaps to dismount, drop the reins and walk ten feet from the horse without his following you. If showing a stock horse, the judge will line up all exhibitors in the center and work each one individually. Your individual work will generally be to figure eight at a lope two or three times, demonstrating ability to change leads correctly. You will then go to the end of the arena coming to a straight, sliding stop. Then turn away from the rail and run to the other end of the arena coming to a straight, sliding stop. Turn again away from the rail and do the same thing, this time stopping at the center of the arena. Then gather your horse and back him in the opposite direction, in a straight line 10 to 15 feet. You will then bring your horse up in front of the judge for your "offsets." With your horse's weight on his hindquarters, and his legs in one position, make a quarter turn to the right, a half turn to the left and a half turn to the right. AHSA rules require him to be in perfect balance, working entirely off his haunches, with head and neck in direct line with body, mouth closed and head at normal height. This is called "dry work." After you have finished your individual work, return to your line up in the center. If showing in an equitation class, you may be asked to also mount and dismount.

If you are showing a cutting horse in "wet work" classes, you will be asked to demonstrate his ability to cut cattle away from the herd by heading a calf in the ring three times in three different directions and then drive him out. Your horse may do this partially with his own body up against the calf, forceably pushing him. We are not concerned with the cutting horse in this book because his work is not generally required of a show horse.

Unless you are showing your hunter in hack classes or in family teams, you will show him individually over jumps in the ring. In hack classes, except as a bridle path hack, you show him at a walk, trot and canter and then selections from the class are made to be shown over two fences three feet and six inches high. In case of working hunter hacks, the judge will select horses apparently the most agreeable to hounds. The main considerations are an even hunting pace, manners, way of going and style of jumping.

If you show your hunter individually or as a team, he will perform over obstacles simulating those found in the hunt field. Under AHSA rules they will be post and rail, chicken coop, Aiken fence, white board fence or gate, brush, stone wall or thorn wall. Your jumps will either have wings or they will be wide enough to be similar to fences in the hunt field. Your jump course may require you to jump both in the ring and outside the ring. The outside course will bring you back into the ring. Generally your hunter will be asked to jump eight fences or four fences twice around.

Naturally, the height and breadth of the jumps will be regulated by the type hunter class in which you are showing, but most of the jumps will be four feet and none exceeding four feet and six inches. Jumps will of course be less for ponies and will be based on the pony's size. The classification generally runs two feet for those 11.2 hands and under, two and one-half feet for those over 11.2 and not exceeding 13 hands, and three feet for those over 13 hands.

When you enter the ring, proceed to your first jump or make a circle before going into the jump. Move him along at a hunting pace and be careful to take the jumps in the correct order. You should have studied the course carefully before the show. If your horse should jump the wrong obstacle, you will be disqualified. If he should refuse a jump, circle him around and present him at the jump again. Should he refuse three times, ride him out of the ring.

If you are showing in a conformation hunter class, after each contestant has shown over the jump course, you will lead your horse into the ring with his saddle removed, to be judged on conformation along with the other contestants. (See Figure 54.) When the selections are made, the ribbons and trophy are given. The ribbon may be placed on the cheek strap of his bridle.

Your mount was judged on conformation, way of going, form and style of jumping and in some cases according to the time he required. A slight touch of the obstacle is not counted against you unless choosing a winner is difficult.

If you are showing a jumper rather than a hunter, there may be some difference in the ring procedure, but you will still show him over the jump course individually.

On entering the ring with your jumper, you are allowed to

make one circle before going into your first jump. You may make this at any gait but must trot, canter or gallop between your obstacles.

You are judged from the time you enter the ring until you have crossed the finish line following the last obstacle.

Your jumper may be scored by AHSA rules or International Equestrian Federation rules, the latter being an international set of rules. The former are by far the most used in this country. Both are contained in the AHSA rule book. The method generally used in scoring is as follows: A hind touch ½ fault; Front touch 1 fault; Knock down with hind portion 2 faults; Knock down with front portion 4 faults; Run-out 4 faults. For a spill, three refusals, or taking the wrong jump, you are disqualified. Ties are run off by raising one or more of the jumps. In some classes you also jump against time.

If you are a good enough equestrian to enter horsemanship classes, your mount in those classes will not be judged. Some of the points considered in judging your horsemanship, besides seat and hands, are posture, how and where your legs are carried, position of your feet in stirrup irons, use of the aids in changing gaits, manner in which your horse is managed and the promptness to obey the commands of the judge or ringmaster. You should show no visible sign of applying your aids when changing your gaits.

Often in horsemanship classes the riders are directed to dismount and exchange horses. This should offer no problem to the pupil who has been taught to ride on several horses. Also, the judge might order figure eights at a canter, stopping on each change of lead, also figure eights at the trot to show change of diagonals. These maneuvers should be practiced by all beginners before entering the show, placing emphasis on mounting, dismounting and backing.

In hunting seat horsemanship classes, contestants may show over jumps as in hunter classes and may also be shown in gaits. Some of the individual requirements in addition to what we have mentioned are to be able to gallop and stop, pull up on turns between fences, jump fences in middle of ring at right angles to the jump course and jump strange horses.

FIG. 54 Conformation Hunter classes require that the hunter shown over jumps must be unsaddled and brought again into the ring to be judged on conformation.

Horsemanship classes for the stock saddle seat differ from the park and hunting seat in that contestants are judged not only on seat and hands but on performance of their horse, his appointments and suitability to rider. The rules stipulate, however, that the performance of the horse is not to be considered more important than the methods used in producing performance. Actually the contestant performs much as he would in a stock horse class.

Index

271